# Cascade Lodge

## The History of a
## North Shore
## Landmark

## by Eugene A. Glader

*Gene Glader*

Previous book by author Eugene Glader: *Amateurism and Athletics*

Published by:          Cascade Lodge

3719 West Highway 61

Lutsen, Minnesota 55612

ISBN:0-9771110-0-8

SAN: 256-7415

First printing July 2005.

Printed in the USA.

# Some Comments about the Book

"This is a wonderful addition to Cook County History! It combines detailed historical documentation with wonderful photos and illustrations of the history of Cascade Lodge—very, very enjoyable reading!"

*Pat Zankman, Cook County Historical society Museum Director.*

"More than the history of one landmark hideaway, the story of Cascade Lodge shows the evolution of Lake Superior's North Shore, from an unforgiving wilderness to one of the Upper Midwest's most enchanting vacation destinations."

*Larry Oakes, Star Tribune of Minneapolis*

"Resorts have and will continue to play a unique role in the future of tourism in Minnesota. The rich and enjoyable history of our resort community, especially along Minnesota's beautiful North Shore, would be lost if not for the efforts of people like Gene Glader. Thanks, Gene, for this great contribution and your family's role in building the wonderful legacy of Cascade Lodge!"

*Dr. Dan Erkkila, University of Minnesota Tourism Center*

"The history of Minnesota's North Shore is a fascinating study of people and nature. The role Cascade Lodge has played in this history is brought to life in this fascinating, well-researched history of one of the North Shore's most storied landmarks. Cascade Lodge will undoubtedly continue to be a major story line as the history of Northen Minnesota continues to unfold."

*Tim Campbell, Northeast Regional Manager, Explore Minnesota Tourism.*

This is a wonderful book. It is rich in history and detail, while proving an easy and enjoyable read. Resorts are part of the essential fabric of Minnesota culture, and your history of this North Shore landmark captures the energy, excitement, dreams, challenges, persistence and ultimately successes of several generations of resorters. Resorts so much reflect the personality of their owners, and this book gives us a sense of each owner as Cascade Lodge develops into a major force among Minnesota resorts. If you have an interest in Minnesota history, have ever dreamt of owning your own resort, or simply want a peek inside one of Minnesota's most cherished industries, this is a must read.

*David Siegel, CAE*
*Executive Vice President, Minnesota Resort & Campground Association*
*President & CEO, Hospitality Minnesota*

## Dedication

This book is dedicated to my wife, Laurene, for sharing with me the work and pleasures of owning and managing a resort. She made the journey worthwhile and a success.

# Contents

# Contents

## Chapter IV
### *The Neudahl's Early Years 1935-1938*

## Chapter V
### *Cascade River State Park History*

# Contents

# Contents

## Chapter IX
### *The Early Glader Years 1981-1989*

# Contents

## Chapter X
## *1990 to the Present*

# Contents

# *Acknowledgements*

No work of this nature is possible without the help and cooperation of others. There have been many people over the years who have provided a picture or bit of information about earlier days at the lodge that have all contributed to making this book a reality. Included in this list are former employees and neighbors that are too numerous to mention. I have also appreciated assistance from the staffs at the Minnesota Historical Museum Library, the St. Louis County Historical Museum Library, the Cook County Historical Museum, the Grand Marais Public Library and the Cook County Recorders Office. Without the cooperation of employees and volunteers in these offices the task would have been impossible.

Some of the other people that provided helpful information were neighbors such as Mr. and Mrs. Gus Johnson and Irving Hanson, who personally knew the Neudahls; and Marilyn Mattson Nyquist, a former employee; and former owners or relatives of former owners such as Mrs. Valaine Robinet, a granddaughter of Mr. & Mrs. Herbert Neudahl, Mrs. JoAnne Rogers House, a daughter of Charles Rogers, Michael and Sharon Rusten, and Carl and Mae Odmark.

A special word of thanks belongs to William Hay for his assistance in locating and interpreting the early property and courts records, Al Hodapp, a former manager of Cascade River State Park, for his help in researching the history of the park and the Spruce Creek CCC Camp, our daughter Sonja Glader Langlie and Pat Ciochetto for editing the manuscript and Jim Ringquist for his skill in editing and restoring the photos and doing the final layout and proofing. A final word of appreciation belongs to my wife, Laurene, for assistance in doing research and for proof reading.

Eugene "Gene" Glader

# Acknowledgements

# Cascade Lodge Time Line

## Some Major dates in Cascade Lodge History

1858 .................... Minnesota became a State.

July 1869 ............. Henry H. Eames purchased land that included the future site of Cascade Lodge from U.S. Government.

March 1874 ........ Minnesota Legislature established Cook County.

1899 .................... Wagon Trail Bridge built over Cascade River.

1916 .................... New bridge constructed over the Cascade River.

November 1916 .. Andrew Haakensen sold the parcel that Eames had purchased to Fred D. McMillen.

June 1922 ............ Edward L. Ogilvie purchased the land on which Cascade Lodge now exists from Fred D. McMillen.

September 1926 .. Morris H. Olson purchased Cascade Lodge from Edward L Ogilvie.

June 1927 ............ Morris H. Olson assigned the lodge to Cascade Lodge, Inc.

August 6, 1927 .... Cascade Lodge Grand Opening.

October 1929 ...... Charles E. Rogers given title to land and buildings at the lodge by stockholders.

August 1931 ........ Gowan-Lenning-Brown filed complaint against Cascade Lodge, Inc.

1932 .................... Current bridge over the Cascade River was completed.

Summer 1934 ...... Mr. & Mrs. Herbert Neudahl managed the lodge.

1934 .................... Minnesota Highway Department purchased approximately 2,300 acres of land along highway and around the mouth of the Cascade River that became Cascade Wayside.

# Time Line

March 1935.........Mr. & Mrs. Herbert Neudahl purchased the lodge.

Summer 1939......Two-thirds of new main lodge opened.

December 1941 to August 1945..........U.S. involved in WWII.

June 1947.............Grand Opening of current Cascade Restaurant building under name of Cascade Inn.

December 1948...Lutsen Ski Area and Sawtooth Mt. Ski Area opened.

1957.....................Cascade Wayside officially became Cascade River State Park.

Summer 1957......West wing of main lodge completed.

Summer of 1957 or 1958 ......... Dining room moved from main lodge to current restaurant building.

Early Sixties........Three unit motel built.

September 1968 ..Herbert F. Neudahl died.

October 1969 ......Michael and Sharon Rusten purchased the lodge from Mrs. Herbert Neudahl.

Winter 1970-71 ...Restaurant opened during the winter for the first time.

July 1981.............Gene and Laurene Glader and Associates purchased the lodge from Michael and Sharon Rusten.

Fall 1990.............New cabins numbers 7 and 12 occupied for first time.

May 2000............New cabin 14 occupied for first time.

Summer 2002......Cascade Lodge Celebrated 75th Anniversary.

May 3, 2004........Michael and Maureen O'Phelan purchased the Lodge from Gene and Laurene Glader.

# *Introduction*

It wasn't long after purchasing the lodge that I became curious about its history and that of the area. I started collecting and saving various pictures and materials about the lodge, thinking that some of this "stuff" should be saved, but not knowing exactly why. I also began to read various books and articles on the history of the county and my interest in the uniqueness of the area grew.

As I learned about the area, my interest in the emergence and development of tourism in the county grew. Over the years I learned various bits of information about some area resorts including the fact that Cascade Lodge was one of the older resorts in the county. As the years passed my wife, Laurene, and I became more emotionally connected to the lodge as we worked with employees, tried to provide a nice vacation spot for guests, and enjoyed the beauty of the area. For us the place became "special" and I began to think about writing some kind of book or booklet about it. As we began to prepare for the 75th Anniversary of the lodge I started to seriously delve into the history of the lodge and decided to write about it.

I began by tracing the history of the parcel of land that became Cascade Lodge back to 1869, when the first recorded transaction involving the land took place. I have woven into the history of the lodge information about such things as modes of transportation, industries and job opportunities in the area, wars, and depressions that had various impacts on the emergence of tourism in the county from that date. No industry stands alone in history. There are always parallel developments. For the tourism industry the development of roads, cars, buses and airplanes certainly parallels the growth of tourism. Many other parallels exist such as the relationship between technology and tourism, the growth of cities and tourism, and the trend toward a shorter work week and tourism. All of these societal factors and others are related to the history of Cascade Lodge and tourism in general. In the chapters that follow, sometimes these parallels will be clearly evident. Other times the relationship will be subtle.

While writing the book I have tried to balance the importance of specific details and interests with the big picture. For some readers, such as people who have been guests at the lodge for years, the details included about buildings and people may be of special interest. For others, these details may be extraneous material, but hopefully the overall story of the lodge and area will be of significant interest. It is also my intention to add to the documented historical record of the county through this book. Hopefully, the balance is appropriate.

In the process of collecting information I was fortunate in being able to contact one daughter of Charles Rogers and grandchildren of the Nuedahls and a few employees who worked at the lodge in the thirties and forties. It was also fortunate that occasionally someone would give us an old picture of the lodge or of members of their family at the lodge. All this was very helpful. I hope readers will be prompted to send us additional information and copies of old pictures and brochures that may shed additional light on the earlier years of the lodge.

Writing the last two chapters of the book, which involves our family's time of ownership has, in some ways, been the easiest part of the lodge's history to describe. We were intimately involved in almost every aspect of the ongoing activities at the lodge and we became part of the history of the place. In addition, we had saved a fair amount of information and pictures from our era. Nevertheless, in many respects this period was the hardest to write because it involves my family and me personally. It has been hard to write about myself and use the word "I".

There is also the risk of lacking objectivity when writing history so soon, especially when one is involved in a project. In spite of these dilemmas I have written about the history of our years at Cascade Lodge to the best of my ability, as I believe my family and I experienced it.

Eugene "Gene" Glader

# The Early History of Cascade Lodge

# Chapter I

## The Beginning

When did Cascade Lodge begin? Nobody knows for sure. Furthermore, determining a date is complicated by questions such as the following: "Did the lodge come into existence when it took in the first guest, or when construction of the buildings began, or when the land was purchased with the intent of starting the lodge?" One could justify the use of any such date as the beginning of the lodge. We have decided to use the date when guests first came to the lodge as its historical beginning. That date is during the summer of 1927, because that is the first time conclusive evidence exists that guests stayed at the lodge. Consequently, 2002 was the year during which we celebrated the 75th Anniversary of the lodge.

During the 1920s the United States was experiencing a booming economy. World War I had ended in 1918 and the general populace was filled with optimism. In Cook County the logging business was thriving and tourism was at the beginning stages of development. Farming and fishing were also significant aspects of the local economy. Since about 1890 thousands of men had come to the area to work in the logging industry, especially during the winters. In the winter they could make snow and iced packed roads across swampy areas and lakes to access inland areas, and for hauling logs out with sleds. This was a practical solution to the accessibility problem. The principle is the same today for loggers with modern tree harvesting machinery.

The exposure of the early loggers to the beauty of the area and its natural resources contributed to the development of tourism as an emerging industry. Many other factors, such as excellent fishing in both Lake Superior and the many inland lakes, good hunting in the surrounding forest, the cooler summer days and evenings, and freedom from hay fever, all brought tourists to the North Shore and Cook County in the twenties and thirties.

The development of tourism in the county parallels the development of various methods of transportation to the area. This parallel continues to the present time and corresponds with the national pattern. Prior to 1916 the major means of traveling to Grand Marais was by ships on Lake Superior. Fishing and logging had opened up many ports along the lake or at least spots where ships would stop off shore in places such as Lutsen, to load and unload people and freight into small boats. Between 1898 and 1928[i] a large network of railroads was developed to support logging from Duluth to Clearwater Lake,[ii] but a railway connection to Grand Marais never materialized even though plans had been made for it.[iii]

**Wagon road bridge over Cascade River built in 1899. The building across the river on the lakeside was the home of the Smulund family. The building on the landside according to a Herb Gibson, son of an early settler, was a store.** *Photo Circa 1910.*

## The Development of Early Roads

In 1879 the *Duluth News Tribune* reported that "Forty miles of the new road has been opened on the Duluth and Pigeon river(sic) wagon road, leaving but twenty miles to be cut in order to open the road for a one-horse team - for winter travel - between Duluth and Grand Marais."[iv] F. B. Hick states that this road was completed eight years later in 1887.[v]

In reality, portions of this road were probably not much more than a walking or one horse trail in the summer and a dog sled trail in the winter. Given the number of rivers and streams flowing into Lake Superior along the North Shore, bridge construction would have been an important factor in the creation of a passable road. A major improvement in travel between Duluth and Grand Marais came in 1899 with the completion of the new bridge over the Cascade River and construction of the final segments of the Lake Shore Road in Lake and Cook Counties.[vi]

The first stagecoach using the new road arrived in Grand Marais on December 19, 1899.[vii] This event truly marked a new era in year-round transportation between Grand Marais and Duluth, and communication with the world for the residents of Cook County.

The first automobile was driven from Duluth to Grand Marais in 1912 and it used the old wagon trail. The *Duluth Herald* newspaper provides some details about the trip. S. R. Kirby, Sr. reports that after they left Beaver Bay "Fully fifteen to twenty windfalls were cleared from the roadway and an equal number the Ford was forced to climb over rather than cut them out. Large boulders caused by the washing away in numerous places were

**Bridge over Cascade River Built in 1916. Note Bridge built in 1899 in the background.** *Photo Courtesy of Dick Eckel.*

apparent everywhere and considerable skill had to be exercised to drive the car through without tearing the axle out or breaking some other part.... On three different occasions steep grades were encountered which were so steep that the gasoline would not flow to the engine from the gasoline tank and the car had to be reversed to get the engine lower than the gasoline tank, and backed up these grades."[viii] In 1916 the new automobile road, Highway 1, was completed between Duluth and Port Arthur, Canada, and a new era of tourism was underway.[ix] Highway 1 was later re-numbered and became Highway 61 in 1934.

### Early Hotels and Resorts

By 1926 and perhaps earlier there were three hotels in Grand Marais: The Sterling Hotel, which is today the East Bay Hotel, the Tourist Hotel, which was originally called the Paine Hotel, and the Arrowhead Hotel. The Tourist Hotel, which burned down in January 1932[x] was on the current site of the Blue Water Cafe. The Arrowhead Hotel was located on the northwest corner of Highway 61 and 1st Ave. West, but is no longer there. In 1927 there were very few resorts in the county, but among those that had come into existence were Lutsen Resort on the North Shore and Clearwater Lodge, Gunflint Lodge and Gateway Resort, which was later renamed Hungry Jack Lodge, on the Gunflint Trail. The Gunflint Trail is a stretch of road approximately 56 miles long that begins in Grand Marais and heads north. About twenty-five miles from Grand Marais and beyond it provides points of access to the Boundary Waters Canoe Area Wilderness. By 1930 the number of resorts in the county had grown to at least eighteen.

### Cascade Lodge and Cascade State Park Land / Early History

The land on which Cascade Lodge is situated is located 100 miles northeast of Duluth and nine miles southwest of Grand Marais in the Arrowhead region of Minnesota. One-fourth of a mile east of the lodge is the Cascade River, aptly named for its beautiful series of waterfalls. Nestled amongst the pines, birch, poplar and maples, which cover the Sawtooth Mountains behind it, the lodge is bordered in front by a vast expanse of Lake Superior, a setting breathtaking in its natural beauty. Wealth of beauty alone, however, is not what prompted the first land speculators' interest. The abstract for the land on which Cascade Lodge is located begins with the issuance of a land patent[1]

---

[1] A patent is "the instrument by which the U.S. Government grants title to public land." Random House Webster's College Dictionary.

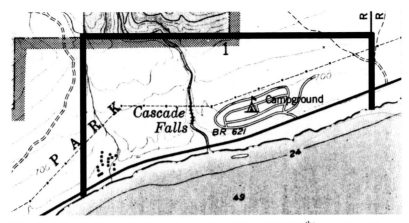

**The dark line indicates the boundary of the 244 and 90/100<sup>ths</sup> acres that Henry Eames purchased in 1869. Note the current location of Cascade Lodge and the park campground.**

dated May 2, 1870 by which Henry H. Eames received ownership of the land from the United States Government. He had actually purchased the land for $306.12 with some type of purchase agreement on July 8, 1869, and was issued the ownership document about a year later on May 2, 1870. Mr. Eames was a geologist from Pennsylvania who had been exploring and prospecting in the Vermillion and North Shore areas.[xi] The purchase included 244 and 90/100<sup>ths</sup> acres, with a west boundary about 200 feet west of the current lodge and an eastern boundary about 7/8<sup>ths</sup> of a mile east of the lodge and a northern boundary about ¼ to ½ mile back from the Lake Superior.[2] This tract of land included the mouth of the Cascade River, its most popular falls, all of the current Cascade River State Park Campground, the trail up to Moose Mt. and more.

The patent for the land was issued the same year that the first three permanent white settlers came to Grand Marais. They were Henry Mayhew, Sam Howenstine and Ted Wakelin.[xii] [3]

During the years that followed, ownership of the land changed several times as speculators purchased various parcels of land in the area. An example of the rapid changing ownership of property was the sale by Henry Eames of an undivided ¾ interest in the land on January 1, 1870 to Robert H. Straham and the remaining ¼ interest to George H. Williams on January 22, 1870. An undivided interest meant that each person owned a certain percentage of the entire parcel.

[2] Legal Description: Lots 1, 2, 3, 4, South Half of NW Quarter of Section 1, Township 60, Range 2, West of the 4<sup>th</sup> P.M.
[3] There is some evidence that the three men came to Grand Marais in 1871 and not 1870.

On November 9, 1874 Lake County[4] put the land up for public auction following a delinquent tax judgment in District Court in St. Louis County. The State of Minnesota either purchased the land at the auction or automatically became the owner, due to the fact that no other bids were received. Earlier in the year, on March 9, 1874 the Minnesota Legislature established Cook County. However, local government of Cook County did not begin until September 7, 1882, when the governor appointed the first county commissioners.[xiii]

In February of 1885, the Minnesota State Legislature legalized the assessment and collection of taxes by officers of Cook County on land in the county that had been forfeited to the State of Minnesota. Thus the land referred to above ended up back in private ownership. It is not clear who the county officials perceived as the owner. In an interesting transaction on August 31, 1885, Richard M. Eames, the son of Henry Eames, gave Hazael Mayhew the Power of Attorney to use or sell an undivided ¼ interest in the same land. This transaction implies that the Eames family must have paid the back taxes and thus been able to regain an undivided ¼ interest in the land. About four years later on, March 21, 1889, the Auditor of Cook County obtained 100% interest in the land from a tax judgment for $10.58 in District Court. On May 6, 1889, the county sold its interest in the land to Thomas W. Mayhew, a brother of Hazael Mayhew. Hazael was the legal first name of the previously mentioned Henry Mayhew.[xiv] Thomas Mayhew had arrived in Grand Marais in 1871, a year after his brother.

Taxes on the same parcel of land became delinquent again in January 1898, and the Cook County Auditor put the land up for sale on May 2, 1898. No bids were received, so Cook County became the owner of the land subject to a three-year redemption period. After the redemption period expired on February 26, 1902, the auditor was allowed to sell the land at a private sale and C.H. Carhart made an offer of $153.50 to the county. On June 11, 1902 he was given a Deed Absolute for the land. This was for the exact 244 and 90/100[ths] acres that Henry Eames had purchased in 1869. About two years later, on December 7, 1904, Mr. and Mrs. Carhart sold the parcel to Mr. & Mrs. Edmund M. Pope through a Quit Claim Deed.[5]

---

[4] Prior to the creation of Cook County the area was part of Lake County, which has its Court House in Two Harbors.

[5] Between Nov. 28, 1902 and Dec. 16, 1904 Mr. & Mrs Carhart went through some legal transactions with the Cook County State Bank involving transferring title to the bank and then back to the Popes. This was probably done to satisfy a loan for which the land was listed as the security.

**Cascade Cabin at Cascade River. Andrew Haakensen is at the right. Note the root cellar, which faced the river.** *Circa 1907.*

**The Cascade Cabin located on the west bank of the Cascade River facing Lake Superior. Martin Haakensen is on the left and on the right is his sister Mrs. Ellen Jacobsen.** *Circa 1908.*

7

**Cascade Cabin on west side of Cascade River. The cabin has been white-washed or had stucco applied since the earlier picture.** *Circa 1912.*

Mr. & Mrs. Edmund M. Pope then sold the land described in the 1869 purchase to Cascade Land & Improvement Company on April 17, 1905. This company was a partnership[6] composed of ten people who each owned a 1/10th interest.[7] Less than a month later, one of the partners, Thelesphar Pronovost, conveyed his 1/10th interest in the land to another company called The Abstract Company. The Abstract Company thus became a partner in the Cascade Land & Improvement Company. The ownership of the Abstract Company is not known.

Andrew Haakensen was another of the ten people who owned a 1/10th interest in the Cascade Land & Improvement Company and he or his relatives built a house on the west side of the Cascade River near its mouth.[8] The building of the house on company land was presumably done with the approval of the Cascade Land and Improvement Company. Sometime between 1910

---

[6] The recorded Quit Claim Deed calls the company a partnership, and the Abstract refers to the company as a corporation, which is a recording error.

[7] The ten partners were Thelesphar Pronovost, Andrew Haakensen, Haakon Spjotvold, Roy Prytz, Mark N. Ralston, Olof Serverson, Mary Bunnell, Ellan A. Humes, Ingebr[e]cht N. Sodalh and Louise Mostue.

[8] There is some evidence that a Herb F. Gibson family built and lived in the house referred to as the Haakensen cabin in the preceding pictures.

and Nov. 25, 1916 Andrew Haakensen became the sole owner of the Cascade Land and Improvement Company and the sole owner of the original parcel of land which Henry Eames purchased from the government in 1869. On November 25, 1916 Haakensen sold the land to Fred D. McMillen, subject to a lease, which allowed Mr. Haakensen and his tenant the use of the house and dock on the west side of the river, with fishing privileges, until May 1, 1917.

Two months prior to the sale of the land to F. D. McMillan the *Cook County News-Herald* reported that McMillan had "completed a primery (sic) survey of the Cascade River for the purpose of considering the possibility of putting in a dam and developing a power plant and furnishing this village and community with electric power and light."[xv] Fortunately, nothing ever came of the idea. Several years later in 1932, the U. S. Army Corps of Engineers conducted a more extensive study of the Cascade River "concerning the possibility of developing this stream for navigation, power development, flood control or irrigation."[xvi] This study was the result of a Rivers and Harbor Act passed by Congress in 1927, which mandated such studies across the nation. Fortunately, the conclusion of the Cascade River study was that it was not practical to develop the river for any of the purposes being considered. Thus ended any consideration for building a dam in the river.

**Fishing shacks and the old bridge at the mouth of Cascade River. The fishing shack on the right was owned by the Smuland brothers.** *Circa 1915.*

The first time that the name of Fred D. McMillen, a land speculator, is found in the abstract of the lodge is March 8, 1909. On that day a Quit Claim Deed dated February 19, 1909 from Richard M. Eames, the son of the original owner of the property, and his wife, was recorded. By this Quit Claim Deed F. D. McMillen was clearing up any ownership rights the Eames family may

The remains of the 1899 wagon bridge over the Cascade River. The east end of the 1916 bridge is at the right side of the photo. Notice that the 1899 bridge is almost at a right angles to the 1916 bridge. The Smuland family home is in the upper left hand corner. The Smuland brothers fishing shack is in the foreground. *Photo courtesy of Norman Smuland, son of Helmer Smuland.*

have had in the original parcel purchased from the government in 1869. As was indicated earlier, the Cascade Land and Improvement Company owned the parcel at this time. Nevertheless, members of the Eames family may have believed that they still had some right to the land. To completely eliminate any claims from the Eames family, Fred McMillen agreed to this contract as part of the process in obtaining ownership of the land.

During the next few months F. D. McMillen followed a similar procedure to clear up any ownership rights that might exist from the heirs of the George

H. William and Robert H. Straham families. Over the next ten years F. D. McMillen continued to acquire and clear title to the land around what is now Cascade Lodge by means of Quit Claim deeds and court judgments. This process culminated with an 11th District Judicial Court Judgment on July 13, 1912 that gave F. D. McMillen title to many parcels of land in the vicinity of Lake Superior and the Cascade River. A few years later, on June 20, 1922, Fred D. McMillen made an application to the 11th Judicial District Court to register the title to the original 244 and 90/100th acre parcel and additional land totaling more than 3,000 acres. Included in this application was the listing of three leases by the following people: Herman Helmerson, Hilmer Smuland and Andrew Trana.[9] [xvii] On the next day, June 21, 1922, Fred. D. McMillen sold to Edward L. Ogilvie of St. Paul, the portion of land that was to become Cascade Lodge.

## The Mouth of the Cascade River

The original route of the Cascade River had the effect of creating a natural little harbor for boats to enter and receive protection from the lake's waves and storms. It also became a natural location for a few fish houses and docks. The original location where the river flowed into Lake Superior was about 80 yards west of the current place where it enters the lake. Originally the river curved to the west as it reached a natural rock wall located at the site of the current bridge, which was built in 1932. The river then flowed west along this rock outcropping for about 80 yards and then turned south again and flowed into the lake. When the highway and bridge were built in 1932, the river was redirected. The original, short, river valley is located just north of the current highway. The site of the original mouth of the river is now a rocky beach area with large boulders placed against the lakeside of the 1916 bridge.

---

[9] Andrew Trana's lease apparently was at the mouth of Spruce Creek according to an interview with Norman Smuland at Cascade Lodge in September, 2003. Norman was the son of Hilmer Smuland.

i   *Frank A. King, <u>Minnesota Logging Railroads</u> (San Marino, California: Golden West Books, 1981), p. 50a.*

ii  *Frank A. King, <u>Minnesota Logging Railroads</u> (San Marino, California: Golden West Books, 1981), p. 95.*

iii *Frank A. King, <u>Minnesota Logging Railroads</u> ( San Marino, California: Golden West Books, 1981), pp. 73-74.*

iv *"The City," <u>Duluth News Tribune</u>, August 15, 1879, p. 4.*

v  *F. B. Hicks,"Historian Tells of Early Beginnings of Grand Marais as an Indian Trading Post," <u>Duluth News Tribune</u>, October 6, 1929, p.12.*

vi *Willis H. Raff, <u>Pioneers in the Wilderness</u> (Grand Marais, Minnesota: Cook County Historical Society, 1981), pp. 303-312.*

vii *"Happenings," <u>Cook County News Herald</u>, December 23, 1899, p. 3.*

viii *S. R. Kirby, Sr., " North Shore Trip in 1912 Not to be Taken Lightly," <u>Duluth Herald,</u> June 20, 1934, p. 8.*

ix *F. B. Hicks,"Historian Tells of Early Beginnings of Grand Marais as an Indian Trading Post," <u>Duluth News Tribune</u>, October 6, 1929, p.12.*

x  *"Grand Marais fire at Its Height", <u>Duluth Herald</u>, January 2, 1932.*

xi *Willis H. Raff, <u>Pioneers in the Wilderness</u> (Grand Marais, Minnesota: Cook County Historical Society, 1981), p.13.*

xii *Steven J. Wright, "Thomas Mayhew: common pioneer, unique man," <u>Duluth News Tribune</u>, February 4, 1979, p.74.*

xiii *F. B. Hicks, "Historian Tells of Early Beginnings of Grand Marais as an Indian Trading Post," <u>Duluth News Tribune</u>, October 6, 1929, p.12.*

xiv *Steven J. Wright, "Thomas Mayhew: common pioneer, unique man," <u>Duluth News Tribune</u>, February 4, 1979, p.74.*

xv *"Survey of Cascade River Made By F. D. McMillan," <u>Cook County News-Herald</u>, September 6, 1916, p. 1.*

xvi *"Letter from the Secretary of War," 73d Congress, 1ˢᵗ Session, House of Representatives, Document No. 77, October 27, 1932.*

xvii *Book 4, Misc., p.239 Cook County Recorders Office, Grand Marais, MN, Application to Register Title.*

**12**

# The Ogilvie Years

# Chapter II

## The Sale of the Site of Cascade Lodge to Ogilvie

The terms of the sale of the land that was to become Cascade Lodge had obviously been agreed upon prior to June 21, 1922. Edward L. Ogilvie was clearly waiting for F. D. McMillen to make application to register the title of the land, which he did on June 20, 1922. Although the contract relating to this sale was never recorded, we do know that a contract was drawn up between them because the contract is referred to in a Warranty Deed, which was drawn up on June 24, 1924, between Fred D. McMillen and Edward L. Ogilvie.[1] The deed indicates that both parties were living in the Twin Cities at the time. The legal description in the Deed is the same as for the current lodge property, which includes 13.68 acres of land. The north boundary of the property follows a quarter section line, but neither the east nor west boundaries are located on any traditional boundary line. It appears that Mr. McMillen and Mr. Ogilvie just agreed on a west and an east point that enclosed the land along what is now called the Cascade Creek and surveyed and measured the line later. Why the sale did not include land at least to the west section boundary or all of lot four in section 1 is surprising.

There is no record of the amount of money that Edward Ogilvie paid for the land, but the fact that a $2.00 Internal Revenue Stamp was attached to the Deed indicates that the price was probably $2,000.00. There is no evidence of any buildings on the property at that time. The sale excluded mineral rights and the land being used for the State Highway. A twenty–five foot wide perpetual right-of-way on the west side of the creek, for use by landowners beyond the property, was also reserved. This right-of-way seems to indicate that Fred McMillen had plans to sell additional parcels of land north of the lodge and further from Lake Superior and to provide access with a road along the creek. On March 27, 1926, Mr. & Mrs. Fred D. McMillen released the right-of-way and highway rights to Edward L. Ogilvie.

The land that the Ogilvies purchased had been surrounded by logging operations in earlier years. Willis Raff, in his book entitled *Pioneers in the Wilderness*, reports that in 1898-99 "C. A. A. Nelson of Lutsen operated a Cedar pole and tie camp near the Cascade River until early April"[i] and in "August of 1899 Fred Sahlberg, of Duluth, set up a camp near 'Carriboo' Point, a mile west of the Cascade River."[ii] Regarding the area east of the river,

---

[1] The Warranty Deed dated June 30, 1924, states that "This conveyance is made pursuant to Contract of June 21, 1922, and in full performance thereof."

Raff writes as follows: "Near the end of the century, the settlers, principally fishermen, had another possible source of winter income: employment in the logging camps that were springing up along the Shore between the Cascade River and Grand Marais. So much work became available indeed that there were periods when some camps had trouble finding men to work in the woods!"[iii] The remains of huge stumps along the current hiking trail going to Lookout Mt. are additional evidence of logging in the vicinity of the lodge during the late 1890's or early 1900's. The stumps are what is left of big white

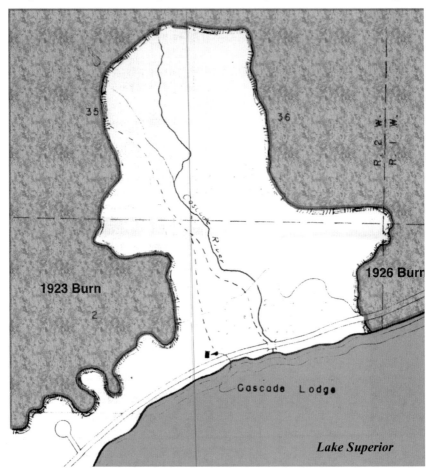

**Firelines showing how close the 1923 and 1926 forest fires came to the lodge and river.** *Map from Cascade River State Park Archives.*

pine and/or cedar trees. Some of these stumps still have visible burn scars, which are most likely from the 1923 forest fire. It was also common to log trees close to the shore of Lake Superior because this allowed for a very short distance to drag or haul logs to the lake, where they could be made into large rafts and towed to sawmills in cities such as Ashland, Wisconsin, and Duluth. Given these factors, it seems reasonable to conclude that many trees were harvested between 1898 and 1922 on the land that was to become Cascade Lodge and Cascade River State Park. This, most likely, would not have been a clear cutting of the area but a selective cutting of big white pines.

## Early Developments at the Lodge

Developing a resort in this very rural setting was no small task. It involved finding solutions for the basic infrastructure items, such as locating a source for good, clean water, building an adequate septic system, clearing trees and stumps, putting in a driveway, and determining the source of energy for heating, lights and cooking. To compound these considerations, electricity from outside sources was not available at Cascade Lodge until at least 1941.[2] It is unlikely that any on-site small generator was used as a source of electricity

**Photo of cabins 1, 2, & 3. Note trees and brush in front of cabins where current driveway is located and the possible electric wires above the cabins.**
*Circa 1923. Photo Courtesy of Nancy Butler.*

[2] In the Nov. 13, 1947 issue of the *Cook County News-Herald,* The Lutsen Light & Power Co. ran a full page ad to celebrate its 7th birthday. In the ad the company states "November 17, 1940, we took over and turned on the electricity for twenty-one customers on four miles of line." Cascade Lodge was beyond the four miles of line.

on the property during the twenties. However, in a 1923 photograph five or six wires from a pole are visible that could possibly have been electric wires from a generator.

**Cabin 11 photo taken in late thirties. Note shed in upper left hand corner, root cellar in back of cabin, chimney on left end of cabin, and lack of railing along creek. The man in the picture is a hunting partner of Ben Klima, who stayed in cabin 11 in the late thirties and early forties to hunt deer.**
*Photo Courtesy of Valinda Littfin, granddaughter of Ben Klima.*

Mr. Ogilvie and his son, Burton, began developing the site into a resort during their first summer of ownership in 1922. Removing trees and stumps, creating a driveway, preparing some building sites, and planning for disposal of sewage were definitely included in the tasks accomplished in the summers of 1922 and 1923. Evidence from photos found by Nancy Butler lend support to the theory that construction of cabins 1, 2, and 3 may have begun in 1922 and were finished or almost finished in 1923.[3]

Burton was most likely on the property during the summer of 1922 and definitely was at the lodge and in charge of the work being done at the site during the summer of 1923. It seems reasonable to assume that Burton lived

---

[3] Nancy Butler has information that her grandfather, Robert B. Kintop, Sr. either built or was part of the crew that worked on the lodge building during 1923.

in what is now cabin 11 during the summer of 1923.[4] This assumption is consistent with information from Edna Johnson.[5] She claims that her Dad, Ben Seglem, and John Skadberg and, perhaps, a third person built the cabin during the winters of 1922-23 and that it was the first building on the lodge property. These men fished on Isle Royale during the summer and worked at the lodge during the winter of 1922-23.[iv] Coincidentally, the summer of 1923 was one of the summers in which a forest fire came quite close to the property.

The root cellar behind cabin 11. The original door was washed away in the July 5, 1999, flood.

It is highly probable that the root cellar in the hillside by Cabin 11 was also built in 1922 or 1923 during Burton Ogilvie's summers at the lodge. Prior to the development of modern refrigeration, root cellars were commonly used for storing perishable foods such as root vegetables and apples. The root cellars kept the food cool in the summer and kept it from freezing in the winter. The cellar still exists and was last used in the early 1980's. Its walls are made of concrete and the inside dimensions are 6 feet wide by 6 1/2 feet long by 5 feet eight inches high with a double door entrance.

[4] See page 24 at the end of this chapter for a current map of the lodge property.
[5] Edna Seglem Johnson worked at the lodge several summers starting in 1934.

**Original main lodge under construction. Note the small building behind and to the left of the lodge. The car has a 1923 license plate.**
*Summer 1923. Photo courtesy of Nancy Butler.*

It also seems reasonable to assume that the Ogilvies began construction on the old main lodge as early as 1922. It is probable that just the foundations and septic system for the original main lodge and some cabins were built at this time.

**Original main lodge under construction with horizontal logs. Summer 1923.**
*Photo courtesy of Nancy Butler.*

Since a supply of good water is essential, not only to every household, but especially to a resort, it is reasonable to speculate that at least one of the two artesian wells on the property was dug and developed during 1922 or 1923. These wells, which still exist, were made of cement tanks buried into

**Original main lodge under construction with chimneys and porch posts in place. Summer or fall 1923. This may have been the status of the lodge when Burton Ogilvie left the lodge in September of 1923.**
*Photo courtesy of Nancy Butler.*

the ground in two locations on the west hillside of the property. Water flowed into the bottoms of these wells and provided a source of good, clean water for the lodge until 1973. By 1973 the artesian wells did not provide enough water for the expanding lodge so a new 300 foot deep well was drilled.

## Ogilvie Puts Lodge Up for Sale

Burton left the lodge in September of 1923 because of illness and moved to California, where he planned to stay. Consequently, Edward L. Ogilvie announced on March 27, 1924, in the *Cook County News-Herald* that because Burton had not fully regained his health, he was giving up his plans to open and operate Cascade Lodge as a summer resort. Edward stated that he was building the lodge primarily for his son and that "He cannot spare the time from his own business to give Cascade Lodge the attention such a place must have and he does not care to continue his interest there when neither he nor his son will be able to give it personal supervision."[v] The same issue of the local newspaper contained an advertisement listing the lodge as under construction and for sale. Developments that could be defined as "under construction" were not listed.

## The Smulund Tragedy

During the autumn following Mr. Ogilvie's announcement to discontinue building the lodge, an event occurred that impacted neighbors living near the mouth of the Cascade River. The tragic incident is a vivid example of the dangers inherent in the commercial fishing industry which involved many local people at the time. Hilmer and Ole Smulund were brothers who fished commercially on Lake Superior. Their harbor and dock location was at the mouth of the Cascade River. The inclusion of Hilmer Smulund in the lease, when Fred D. McMillen made an application to register the title to the land in 1922, confirms that he lived in a house near the river. On Thanksgiving Day, 1924, the Smulund brothers both drowned while setting their nets. Hilmer was married, the father of six children, and was about 40 years old. Ole was single and a couple of years younger. The newspaper account of the accident is as follows:

20

"Last Thursday afternoon, Hilmer and Ole Smulund, fishermen at Cascade, went out upon the lake to set nets and had heavy sand bags,[6] weighing 400 pounds each, in the boat with which to weight (sic) down the nets so that they would withstand the heavy seas.

"The deduction made from appearances are that Ole was the first to get into the water, the supposition being that the rope attached to a sand bag became tangled around his wrist, and when the bag was rolled into the lake it pulled him with it, and down to the bottom. Hilmer tried to save him, first pulling off his boots, which were in the boat, and plunging beneath the surface in an attempt to release his brother. Before making the hazardous venture he tied a rope, attached to a float on the nets, around his wrist and he probably floated in the icy water for some time, as there was no water in his lungs, while Ole's lungs were filled and he was bloated.

"Other fishermen were out in the lake beyond where the Smulunds were fishing, but it is hard to see against the shore this time of year, and consequently they were not seen. And that is one sad part of the tragedy, else they might have been saved.

"There is a bond of sympathy among fishermen which was exemplified by the way they turned out to help when a call of distress was sent along the shore. Volunteers were out with their boats all night, looking for the men who had failed to return by nightfall, hoping that they were still afloat and alive, waiting to be saved. As soon as day broke, the bodies were recovered. Ole was enmeshed in the net, and Hilmer was found by the float fastened by a rope to his wrist."[vi]

## The Sale of the Lodge to Morris H. Olson

On September 21, 1926, two and one-half years after he decided to sell the lodge, Edward L. Ogilvie sold the property to Morris H. Olson for $11,000.00 by Contract for Deed. According to the Consumer Price Index, this was equivalent to $112,175.00 in the year 2002. The agreement included a cash down payment of $4,000.00 with payments of $1,500.00 for two years, and payments of $2,000.00 the third and fourth years. As part of the Contract for Deed, Morris Olson was obligated to insure against loss by fire and lightning and for the improvements on the land for not less than $7,000.

---

[6] Norman Smuland, the son of Hilmer claims that they and other fishmen were using rocks for weights at this time. He claims that the use of sand bags came later. Norman spells his name with an "a" in Smuland; whereas the newspaper account of the drowning spelled Smulund with a "u."

The obligation to insure the improvements is another indication that some buildings had been built or were under construction on the site. Since the lodge was open for guests in the summer of 1927, it seems reasonable to conclude that the original main lodge and some cabins were near completion by the fall of 1923 when Burton Ogilvie left the lodge in September of that year. It is very probable that Charles Rogers added the vertical log sections to the front of the main lodge in 1927. This theory is supported by conversations with Charles Rogers' daughter, JoAnne, who recalls her Dad talking about building with logs, including vertical logs, at the lodge.

On October 14, 1926 the *Cook County News-Herald* stated that Morris Olson had bought Cascade Lodge and predicted that "The lodge will doubtless be a very popular summer resort."[vii] Morris Olson was a local businessman who owned the North Shore Garage and The Motor Inn,[viii] which was the Ford dealership in Grand Marais. In June of 1927 he was elected Secretary of the new Grand Marais Business Men's Club.[ix] He was also a Director of the Grand Marais State Bank.[x]

**Early End View of Original Main Lodge. Circa 1927.**
*Photo Courtesy of JoAnne Rogers House.*

On October 6, 1926, a few days after the sale of the property to Morris H. Olson, the Articles of Incorporation for Cascade Lodge, Inc. were notarized.[xi] The three people forming the corporation were Morris H. Olson of Grand Marais, Minnesota, Charles E. Rogers of Forest Lake, Minnesota, and Everett G. Tufts of Grand Marais, Minnesota. The first officers of the corporation were established as follows: Morris H. Olson, President; Charles E. Rogers, Vice President; and Everett G. Tufts, Secretary and Treasurer. Article I of the corporation stated that "The principal place of transacting business of this corporation shall be at Cascade," clearly indicating that the intent of the corporation was to purchase Cascade Lodge. The corporation had the Contract for Deed, by which Morris Olson had purchased the lodge, assigned to Cascade Lodge, Inc., on June 1, 1927. Thus began Cascade Lodge, an historic North Shore resort.

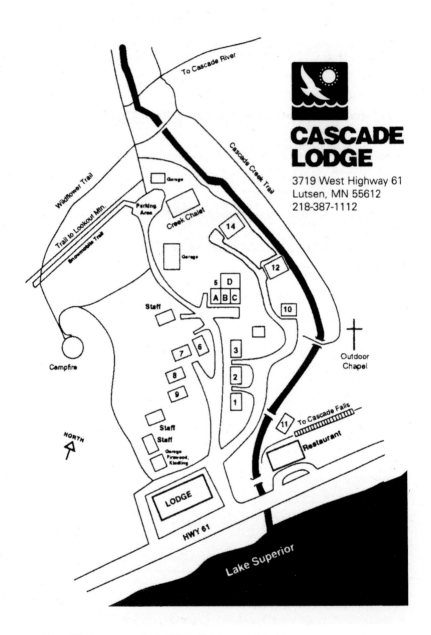

**Map of lodge property in 2002. Cabins are listed by current number.**

[i] *Willis H. Raff, Pioneers in the Wilderness, (Grand Marais, MN: Cook County Historical Society, 1981), p. 120.*

[ii] *Willis H. Raff, Pioneers in the Wilderness, (Grand Marais, MN: Cook County Historical Society, 1981), p. 120.*

[iii] *Willis H. Raff, Pioneers in the Wilderness, (Grand Marais, MN: Cook County Historical Society, 1981), p. 119.*

[iv] *Interview with Edna Seglem Johnson on June 15, 2002.*

[v] *"Cascade Lodge for Sale," Cook County News-Herald, March 27, 1924, p. 1.*

[vi] *"Drowned In Lake Superior Thanksgiving," Cook County News-Herald, December 4, 1924, p.1.*

[vii] *"New-ettes of Grand Marais and Vicinity," Cook County News Herald, October 14, 1926, p. 4.*

[viii] *"New-ettes of Grand Marais and Vicinity," Cook County News Herald, December 1, 1921, p. 6.*

[ix] *"Business Men's Club Organizes," Cook County News-Herald, June 16, 1927. p. 1.*

[x] *Henry P. Peterson, "Grand Marais: the Last big Outpost of the Arrowhead," The Duluth News Tribune, August 23, 1927, p. 12.*

[xi] *"Certificate of Incorporation of Cascade Lodge," Cook County News-Herald, October 21, 1926, p.5.*

The Ogilvie Years

# The Charles Rogers Era 1927-1935

# Chapter III

## The New Lodge Owners

During the early summer of 1927, the new owners Morris H. Olson, Charles E. Rogers and Everett G. Tufts opened Cascade Lodge for business. As was mentioned in the previous chapter, Morris H. Olson was a prominent Grand Marais businessman. Everett G. Tufts, was also a Grand Marais businessman and owned the Motor Inn Garage.[1] The garage sold canoes, boats and engines for boats and most likely repaired automobiles.[i] Charles E. Rogers was a young man from Forest Lake, Minnesota who enjoyed the beauty and wildlife of the North Shore. He was only 26 years old when he became Vice President of Cascade Lodge, Inc. in 1926.

Unfortunately, all members of Charles E. Rogers' family died when he was just a young man. His father died in 1911 from tuberculosis, a brother, Elmer, died of tuberculosis some time after his father died and his mother passed away in 1918. This left Charles alone at the age of 18, but not without some financial resources.[ii] While living in Forest Lake, Charles' father was involved in the firm of Winston & Deer, a contractor in the mining town of Hibbing, Minnesota. It is through this involvement that his father accumulated some financial resources.[iii] Charles attended St. Thomas Academy for three years and graduated in 1923. Then he attended St. Thomas College for two and one-half years from September 1923 through December 1925.[iv] One can only speculate as to how he met Morris Olson and Everett Tufts in Grand Marais.

## The Lodge Opens for Business

The exact date that guests began coming to the lodge for lodging and meals is not known, but it was probably in June of 1927. It is known that a dance was held at the lodge on July 30th. The following week the *Cook County News-Herald*, the local weekly newspaper, reported that a large crowd had attended and that the dance was a big success.[v] Then came the big event of the summer, the official Grand Opening of Cascade Lodge on August 6, 1927.

For this event an advertisement about one-third of a page in size was placed in the *Cook County News-Herald*.[vi] The ad stated that "All the Latest Dance Hits by the 'Toe Ticklers' The Snazzy, Jazzy Five" would perform.

---

[1] Not to be confused with the Motor Inn owned by Morris H. Olson mentioned in the previous chapter.

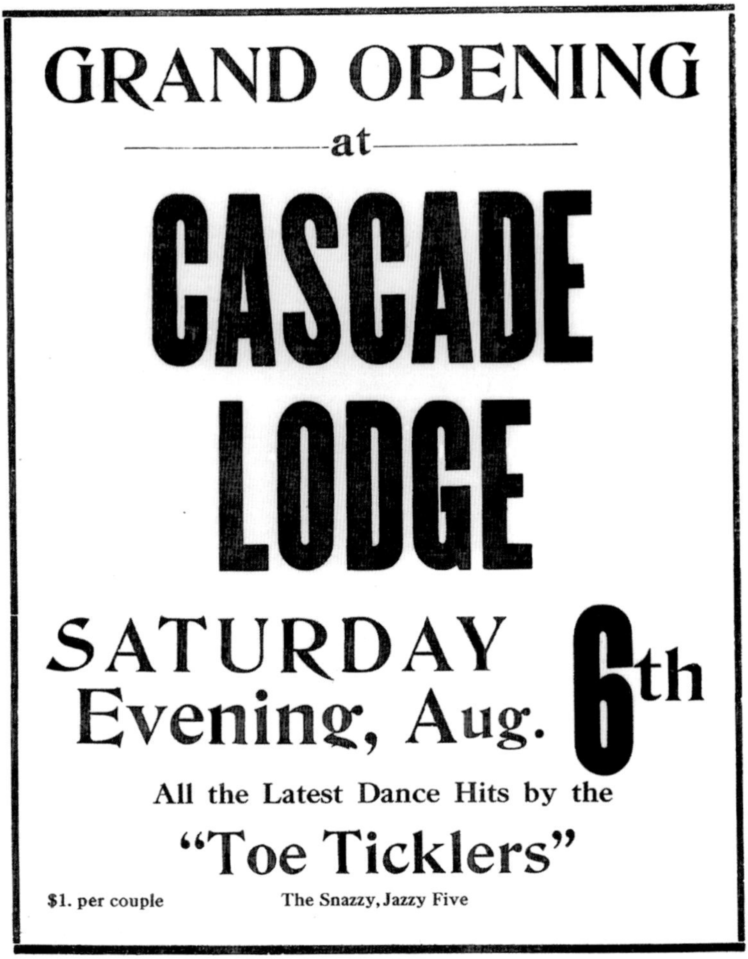

**GRAND OPENING**

——at——

# CASCADE LODGE

## SATURDAY
## Evening, Aug. 6th

All the Latest Dance Hits by the

## "Toe Ticklers"

$1. per couple          The Snazzy, Jazzy Five

**Advertisement in *Cook County News-Herald* on August 4, 1927. About one-third page in size.**

Throughout August of that first summer, dances at the lodge were promoted every Saturday night. However, there are no advertisements for dances again at Cascade Lodge in the local newspaper for almost five years.

Records are not absolutely clear, but most likely Charles Rogers managed the lodge during the first summer. A brief article in the *Cook County News-Herald* announcing the opening of the lodge on June 10th for the 1928 season would seem to imply that Rogers was the manager in 1927. The article states that " Charles Rogers will be on hand to meet you with a smile and see that every one of your wants are attended to."[vii] At the least this confirms that Charles E. Rogers was the manager in the summer of 1928 and it has already been established that the other corporation officers had their own businesses to manage. In addition, Rogers' daughter, JoAnne, claims that her dad worked at the lodge during the early days and recalls her dad saying that he built or helped build the log cabins at the lodge.[viii]

**The earliest photo of the finished original main lodge. Note the size of the spruce trees in front of the lodge. The same trees are located by the play area today.** *Circa 1927. Photo courtesy of JoAnne Rogers House.*

It was pointed out in the previous chapter, that the cabin now called cabin 11 was constructed between 1922 and 1923. There is no clear documentation as to when cabins 1, 2, and 3 were actually finished. We know that construction of the cabins was begun by the Ogilvies and they may have been finished by Charles Rogers. Whether one or all three of the cabins were ready for occupancy by the summer of 1927 is not clear. From old photos it does appear that cabin 1 was finished before cabins 2 and 3. Furthermore, it is highly unlikely that any cabins were built between 1930 and 1935 when the lodge experienced financial difficulties.

**Cabins 1, 2, and 3 located on the right of the main driveway into the lodge.** *Circa 1936. Photo courtesy Valaine Robinet, granddaughter of Mr. & Mrs. Nuedahl.*

It appears that the lodge was only open for about three months each summer during the early years. This schedule is supported by the fact that Charles Rogers was owed wages for only three months work in 1930 and 1931 according to his claim in the court case that is mentioned later in this chapter. A typical schedule for a resort of that era was to be open from Memorial Day to Labor Day or from the opening day of fishing season until Labor Day. On March 1, 1928 Charles was married to Ruth E. Richeleau from Wyoming, Minnesota[ix] and she joined in operating the lodge. They resided in Duluth during the winter months.

## The Local Economy in the late Twenties and early Thirties

The lodge opened during a period of prosperity and growth for Grand Marais and the nearby areas. Evidence of this economic growth is the fact that in January 1924 a daily bus began traveling from Grand Marais to Duluth and back to Grand Marais.[x] By December 1925 a truck hauling freight was making the trip to Duluth twice a week and by July 1926 was making trips on a daily basis. Other evidence of growth in the Cook County economy was the steady, but slow, growth in population. This growth is illustrated by the following chart.

**Fireplace in Original Main lodge.** *Circa 1927.*

## Population of Grand Marais and Cook County[2]

| Year | Grand Marais | Cook County[xi] |
|------|------|------|
| 1880 | Not Available | 65 |
| 1890 | Not Available | 95 |
| 1900 | Not Available | 810 |
| 1910 | 355 | 1336 |
| 1920 | 443 | 1841 |
| 1930 | 618 | 2435 |
| 1940 | 855 | 3030 |

Even though the year-round population of Grand Marais and Cook County was relatively low in the twenties and thirties, the number of seasonal workers and tourists was significant. This fact is supported by the number of new hotels and resorts that were developed in Cook County during these two decades.

### Signs of Financial Trouble at Cascade Lodge, Inc.

On October 29, 1929 the economic boom on Wall Street began to crumble and the United States entered its long, painful depression period. Cascade Lodge and Cook County were not immune from the financial downturn of the economy. The first evidence of financial uncertainties at Cascade Lodge was the failure of the Corporation or Morris Olson, the corporation president, to make the $2,000.00 payment due to Edward L. Ogilvie on September 21, 1929. This happened one month before "Black Friday" on Wall Street. Failure to make the payment, when just a few months earlier in May of 1929, Olson had the money to join the exclusive Naniboujou Club,[3] epitomizes the dramatic downturn in the economy.[xii] This failure to make the payment is recorded in a "Notice of Vendee of Cancellation of Contract Conveyance of Real Property" on October 4, 1929 from Edward Ogilvie to Morris Olson.[xiii] The notice gave Morris Olson 30 days to make the payment or his interests in the property would be terminated. A key factor to take note of in these proceedings is that even though Morris Olson had assigned to Cascade Lodge, Inc., the Contract for Deed between him and Edward Ogilvie, he could still have protected

---

[2] It is probable that the census figures before 1924 do not include all the Native Americans, because Indians on reservations were not citizens until 1924, and 19th and early 20th century census takers did not count Indians for congressional representation.

[3] The Naniboujou Club was an exclusive club located about 15 miles east of Grand Marais, near Hovland, MN.

his interest in the corporation by paying Edward Ogilvie out of his personal resources if the corporation failed to make the payment.

At the time, Cascade Lodge, Inc. owed Charles E. Rogers, Vice President of the corporation, a large amount of money and, according to the filed affidavit, Rogers was unwilling to make further advances directly to the corporation.[xiv] He was however, willing to solve the problem of the payment due to Edward Ogilvie, by agreeing to make the $2,000.00 plus interest payment directly to Mr. Ogilvie from his own personal resources. At the same time, the three officers of the corporation agreed that Charles E. Rogers would take title to the Cascade Lodge real property (buildings and land) in his own name, and that he would convey the property title back to Cascade Lodge, Inc. when and if the corporation paid its entire indebtedness to him. This agreement or transaction, however, was not filed with the county until March 21, 1935. Consequently, Cascade Lodge, Inc., to which the purchaser's interest in the Contract for Deed had been assigned in 1927, remained the recorded owner of the business and property until March 21, 1935.[xv]

On October 6, 1930, Charles Rogers made the fourth and final payment on the Contract for Deed and Mr. and Mrs. Edward L. Ogilvie issued a Warranty Deed to him for the lodge property. Recording this transaction was also neglected and it wasn't until March 21, 1935 that it was officially recorded in the Court House.

Consequently, Charles E. Rogers became the sole owner of the real property known as Cascade Lodge, but Cascade Lodge, Inc. remained the owner of record in the Court House and the apparent owner of the business. It is worth noting that earlier in the year on February 11, 1930, Everett G. Tuffs and Morris H. Olson, the other two officers of Cascade Lodge, Inc. had signed a note stating that the corporation owed Rogers $12,099.88.[xvi] The note was for cash advances to the corporation, auto and gas expenses paid for by Charles Rogers and unpaid salary. There does not appear to have been any agreement between the three corporate officers regarding ownership of the business if Rogers did not get paid. Perhaps everyone was still optimistic about recouping their investments in the lodge.

Obtaining short term or long term loans from banks was very difficult during this period. Consequently, almost the entire financing for the development of the lodge and its operating expenses had to be personally assumed by the owners. The only evidence of bank financing involved during these early years was a loan of $668.60 by the Grand Marais State Bank to Cascade Lodge, Inc. and guaranteed by Charles Rogers.

## Highway 1 Upgraded

In spite of the poor economy, one positive development for the lodge and other area businesses during the early thirties, was the major rebuilding and upgrading of Highway 1. The importance of good roads to the emerging tourism industry in northern Minnesota is apparent by the listing of several highway improvement projects in the Minnesota Arrowhead Association's annual report of 1931.[4] This report states that 11.2 miles of Highway 1 northeast of Duluth were graded and graveled in 1931 and 20.4 miles of grading was under contract for 1932.[xvii]

Earlier, in March of 1930, the Minnesota Highway Department announced that it was planning to blacktop a 29 mile section of Highway 1 from Beaver Bay to Schroeder and a 25.3 mile stretch from Two Harbors to Beaver Bay. [xviii] The highway between Tofte and Grand Marais was rebuilt during 1932 and 1933[xix], with blacktop applied to much of this area in 1933.[xx] The new bridge over the Cascade River was finished in 1932 as part of the highway improvement project. The result was a totally new and blacktopped highway from Duluth to Grand Marais by about the fall of 1933. As part of the design and planning for the new highway the State of Minnesota acquired a one hundred foot right-of-way for the highway across the lodge property on September 24, 1930. That same right-of-way exists today.

**1916 bridge over Cascade River being filled in underneath after 1932 bridge was finished.** *Photo from CCC archives.*

---

[4] The Minnesota Arrowhead Association was a significant promotional organization for tourism in Northeastern Minnesota.

The road improvements were probably a blessing and a curse for Cascade Lodge during 1932 and 1933. Just as today, every section of the highway that is improved is a great asset to tourism businesses. Temporary negatives are the disruptions and dust occurring in front of a business during construction. Regarding Cascade Lodge, it is not known if the road improvements were helpful or detrimental to the lodge during the difficult years of 1931 through 1933.

## Financial Difficulties Continue at the Lodge

Although Charles Rogers had made the final payment to Edward Ogilvie in 1930 and now held a Warranty Deed for the lodge, the depression continued to have a negative effect on tourism and consequently on lodge finances. Apparently it was impossible for the lodge to keep current with some of its start up and ongoing expenses. For example Edwin Nunstedt, who owned the Builder's Supply Company in Grand Marais claimed in a Mechanic's Lien that the lodge owed him $84.20 for materials delivered on May 23, 1929 and on January 10, 1934.[xxi]

The next evidence of financial difficulty came on August 14, 1931 when the Gowan-Lenning-Brown Co. filed a complaint against Cascade Lodge, Inc. in the Second Judicial District Court in Ramsey County for $313.46, which was owed the company.[xxii] Henry E. Horwitz was the attorney for the Gowan-Lenning-Brown Co. and an Edward A. Knapp represented Cascade Lodge Inc. The Gowan-Lenning-Brown, Co. was a wholesale grocery company in Duluth that sold groceries to resorts and restaurants in the Grand Marais area. The complaint asked the court to sequester the assets of Cascade Lodge, Inc. and to appoint a receiver of the property. The complaint was docketed in Cook County on or about August 24, 1931.[xxiii] Less than five months later, on January 9, 1932 the judge ordered all assets, property, and corporate stock to be sequestered and appointed Henry E. Horwitz the receiver with all powers and authority of a receiver under the law at that time.

The end result of sequestering the assets of Cascade Lodge, Inc. was in effect the equivalent of what today would be called a forced filing of bankruptcy by the corporation. By means of the Court Order Henry E. Horwitz had full authority to handle the business and legal affairs of the lodge as of January 9, 1932. Any plan of the corporation or hope of regaining ownership of the lodge if the corporation could pay off its indebtedness to Charles Rogers based on its settlement with Rogers on October 6, 1930 became highly unlikely as of

**34**

1932. Apparently by 1932 Morris Olson and Everett Tufts were unable to help with problems faced by the corporation and left all the decisions in the hands of Charles Rogers. It is known that Morris Olson was still on the Board of Directors of the Grand Marais State Bank as of January 1931,[xxiv] but not after January 5, 1932.[xxv] When he sold his Ford dealership is not certain, but it was before 1935. Whether he had moved away from the area by 1932 is unknown. The local paper never mentions anything about Everett Tufts after about 1929.

Why an attorney for the plaintiff, the Gowan-Lenning-Brown Co., would be appointed the receiver seems somewhat irregular. This decision is further complicated by the fact that by 1935 and perhaps earlier, Edward A. Knapp, the original attorney for Cascade Lodge, Inc. became the attorney for Henry E. Horwitz, the receiver. However, there is no evidence that Charles Rogers had any objections to these decisions.

In understanding the court case a key distinction to keep in mind is that the complaint was filed against Cascade Lodge, Inc. and not against Charles Rogers or the other corporation shareholders. Nevertheless, it is perplexing why Charles Rogers either could not or chose not to pay the $313.46 bill and thus avoid the court proceeding. He had invested five years of his life in the lodge, plus thousands of dollars by 1932, owned the real estate, and had a lot at stake. It seems highly unlikely that Rogers would not have personally paid the $313.46 bill to the Gowan-Lenning-Brown, Co. if he had realized that the lodge was going to be tied up in a receivership for several years due to a suit against Cascade Lodge, Inc. Since it is not known why the court process was allowed to go forward, the situation raises other questions such as the following: (1) Were all of the officers of the corporation so strapped for cash that they could not come up with $313.46? It is worth noting that, according to the Consumers Price Index, the amount was the equivalent of about $4,352.00 in year 2002 currency. (2) Was the credit rating of the corporation and individuals such that the local bank refused to help them at this point or was the financial status of the bank such that they could not help them?

Since the three officers of the corporation agreed that Rogers would take title to the Cascade Lodge real property (buildings and land) in his own name, combined with the fact that he had made the final payment on the Contract for Deed, he may not have seen the lawsuit as a threat to his interests. In fact he may have viewed the lawsuit as a means of receiving payments for the money owed to him by the corporation. From reading the court documents it seems clear that Charles Rogers viewed himself as more of a claimant against Cascade Lodge, Inc. than a defendant of the corporation.

A highly probable scenario is that Charles Rogers thought that he owned all the lodge property, equipment and supplies based on the agreement he had entered into with the corporation in 1929. In fact it may have been the intent of the corporation officers to include everything related to the operation of the lodge in the agreement. This may explain the absence of Morris Olson and Everett Tufts, the other two corporation officers, in the court proceedings. However, the court ruled that Charles Rogers owned only the land and buildings and not the supplies and equipment for operating the resort.

Charles and Ruth Rogers were also raising their young family during these early depression years. Their first child, Henrietta, was born on July 7, 1930. Their second child, JoAnne was born on November 4, 1931 and their third child, Charles was born in on December 26, 1932. According to JoAnne Rogers House, her mother intensely disliked living at the resort. This was partly because she had to care for the small children in rather rustic conditions.[xxvi]

Most likely the Rogers lived in what is now cabin 11 or some other staff cabin during their summers at the lodge. The possibility of the Rogers having personal living space in the old main lodge is ruled out by the clear recollection of Mrs. Edna Seglem Johnson that there were no bedrooms in the old main lodge for staff members or guests.[xxvii]

Perhaps Mrs. Ruth Rogers' dislike of living at the lodge, combined with the financial stress involved in operating the lodge during the depression, resulted in Charles Rogers wanting out of the business. It is also possible that Rogers simply saw the court proceeding as a way to dissolve the corporation under difficult circumstances. Perhaps the other corporation officers, Morris Olson and Everett Tufts decided to abandon their investment in Cascade Lodge, Inc. and let Rogers deal with the corporate affairs. Or Perhaps Olson and Tufts thought that the bills were Rogers' since he was managing the lodge. If Rogers had tried and failed to arrive at some mutually acceptable terms with Olson and Tufts for purchasing their shares in the corporation, the court process would make more sense. The court documents and processes seem to support these possibilities, but one can only speculate about such scenarios.

It is clear that the court viewed Charles Rogers as the owner of the buildings and land at the lodge, but the corporation as the owner of the goods in the lodge, such as towels, silverware, dishes, linens, furniture and equipment. In hindsight it seems clear that Charles Rogers should have had Morris Olson and Everett Tufts, the other corporation stockholders, also convey the furnishings and equipment to him on October 1929 when they transferred the corporations interest in the real property to him. That may, in fact, have been their intention; however, the document used the term "real property" which typically means land and buildings. It is also possible that Olson and Tufts wanted to maintain the corporation's ownership of the furnishings and the business as a possible means of recouping their investments. They had all invested money in the corporation and obviously no one wanted to lose his investment.

It would also appear that Charles Rogers should have had the Warranty Deed he received from Mr. Ogilvie recorded immediately. The failure to record the purchase of the Contract for Deed in October 1929, the Warranty Deed in October 1930 and the transfer of ownership of the lodge to Charles Rogers from the corporation in 1929, resulted in all the property being put into receivership by the court in 1932.

Even though the lodge was in receivership from January 9, 1932 until March 15, 1935 there is no evidence that the lodge did not open each summer during this time. It seems safe to assume that Charles Rogers continued to manage the lodge during the summers of 1932 and 1933. It is known that at least one dance was promoted at the lodge in 1932[xxviii] and that several dances were promoted during July and August of 1933.

While under receivership, the business would have been operated for the benefit of the receiver. Consequently, any net income would have belonged to the receiver. However, wages to Rogers would have been a legitimate expense. The court records do not include any information about income and expenses at the lodge during this period.

**BIG**

**DANCE**

at Cascade Lodge
July 16th

Given by — Martin Sagdalen

*Music by*
North Shore Aircooled
Orchestra

TICKETS 50c

## Neudahls First Lease and then Purchase the Lodge

According to Charles Rogers' daughter JoAnne, the family moved back to Forest Lake in 1933 where Charles still owned the house and land where he had grown up. The move most likely took place after the 1933 tourist season. We do know that in the spring of 1934 Mr. and Mrs. Herbert Neudahl, the future owners of the lodge, leased the lodge and became the managers for the 1934 season. The lodge and restaurant were fully operational at this time.[xxix] Possibly they leased the lodge from Charles Rogers, with the approval of the receiver. In retrospect, it appears that the Neudahls were interested in buying the lodge at this point, and all parties were willing to lease the lodge to them for a summer, perhaps as a way for them to take a serious look at the business. It is not known whether the Neudahls had ever been guests at the lodge or how they learned that it was for sale.

**Old Main Lodge and cabins 1, 2 and 3 on the right. Note height of the trees in front of the lodge. Also note the cabin located on what is now the parking area in front of the motel.** *Circa 1935 or 1938.*

On December 20, 1934 Henry E. Horwitz, the receiver, Mr. & Mrs. Charles E. Rogers and Mr. & Mrs. Herbert F. Neudahl all signed a notarized sales agreement. By means of this agreement the Neudahls agreed to pay $8,000.00 for the lodge. Out of the $8,000.00 an amount of $1,000.00 for personal property owned by Cascade Lodge, Inc. and located in the buildings known as Cascade Lodge was to go to the receiver.[5] The Rogers were also to receive from the Neudahls a house, with furnishings, and land in Anoka County.[6] On

---

[5] The Agreement is included in the court documents.
[6] Legal description: The East forty (40) feet of Lots Twenty-four (24) A and B, Twenty-five (25) A and B, and Twenty-six (26) A, in Block Seventy (70) of Coon Lake Beach Third Map.

**38**

January 19, 1935 Henry E. Horwitz petitioned the court to approve the sale. In the record of the petition it is clear that there was not total agreement by all parties regarding the value of the personal property. Nevertheless, the court was urged to approve the sale. The petition states "That the time element in said transaction is of great importance for the reason that said transaction must be completed promptly in order to retain the proposed purchaser; that Charles E. Rogers is afraid of losing his customer for the real property if there is much delay and for that reason is willing to permit Cascade Lodge [Inc.] to receive one Thousand Dollars ($1,000) of the proceeds of said sale."[xxx] In understanding the previous quotation it is important to remember that Charles Rogers was a creditor in the suit against Cascade Lodge, Inc. Therefore, the $1,000.00 that was to be paid to Cascade Lodge [Inc.], was the source of funds from which the court costs and creditors were to be paid.

Among those present at the hearing was Charles E. Rogers, who was both a stockholder of the corporation and a creditor. Others present were "Grand Marais State Bank and Edwin Nunstedt, two of the creditors of Cascade Lodge appeared by their attorney J. Henry Elliasen, and Herbert F. Neudahl and Minnie E. Neudahl, his wife, appearing by their attorney Arthur R. Schutte, there being no other appearances."[xxxi] Since no one at the hearing objected to the petition to sell the lodge, on January 25, 1935 the court issued an Order that Henry E. Horwitz, as receiver of Cascade Lodge, Inc. be granted the authority to negotiate a sale with Charles Rogers, including specified personal property in the lodge.[xxxii] The intent of the order implies that Mr. Horwitz was to negotiate a sale to Mr. and Mrs. Herbert Neudahl involving Charles Rogers. Questions such as the following seem reasonable: Did the Neudahls personally know Henry E. Horwitz or Charles Rogers and thus learn about the suit by the Gowan-Lenning-Brown Company? Were the Neudahls pursued as potential buyers of the lodge by Charles Rogers? The answers to these questions will probably never be known. What is known is that the sale of the lodge to Mr. & Mrs. Neudahl took place on March 14, 1935 and was recorded on March 21, 1935 in the Cook County Court House.

The terms of the sale involved having the Neudahls pay $1,000.00 for personal property belonging to Cascade Lodge, Inc. This money was given to Mr. Horwitz, as the receiver, to cover his office expenses and fees. The court approved $427.80 for such fees and ordered that the balance of $572.20 be disbursed among the creditors.[xxxiii] The only creditors at the end of the court proceeding were the following: (1) Fitger Brewing Company,

Duluth, Minnesota for $25.30, (2) Ruth Gilbertson, Grand Marais, Minnesota for $15.00 for payment on a piano, (3) Northwestern Bell Telephone Co., Grand Marais, Minnesota for $23.83 and (4) Charles E. Rogers, Forest Lake, Minnesota for $20,054.08. Consequently, after the other creditors were paid, Mr. & Mrs. Charles Rogers received $508.07 from this distribution. Mr. & Mrs. Rogers received $7,000.00 for the land and buildings[7] and a house, with some furnishings, and five lots in Anoka County as part of the transaction. Charles Rogers had apparently satisfied all other creditors. Thus began a new chapter in the history of Cascade Lodge on March 14, 1935 with Herbert and Minnie Neudahl as the new owners.

Charles Rogers later built a beautiful log home on Forest Lake, which unfortunately burned to the ground in 1955. In addition to the loss of this home, almost all the family owned pictures and documents from the Charles Rogers' years at Cascade Lodge were lost. In January of 1966, Charles Rogers was visiting the North Shore, which he loved, and while eating at Mabel's Cafe in Grand Marais on January 6th he choked to death on some food.

Charles Rogers, Morris Olson and Everett Tuft are to be commended for the tremendous task they undertook in opening a lodge that was to become a landmark on the North Shore. They took on a huge task during some very difficult times. Charles Rogers, as the manager and perhaps the biggest investor, and certainly the person who put in the most work on the project, deserves a great deal of credit for all that was accomplished.

---

[7] $500.00 was paid to the Rogers at the time of signing the sales agreement, and $2,500.00 was paid to them when the court approved the sale. At the time the court approved the sale the Nuedahls also gave the $1,000.00 to the receiver. For the remaining $4,000.00 a mortgage was arranged with the Nuedahls requiring payment to Mr. & Mrs. Charles Rogers of $500.00 plus interest every six months for four years.

[i] *"Motor Inn Garages Ad," Cook County News-Herald, May 20, 1926, p. 3.*

[ii] *Cliff Buchan, "Builder left mark with lakeshore log homes," Forest Lake Times, Feb. 6, 2003, pp. 1 & 12.*

[iii] *"Passed to the Great Beyond," The Forest Lake Advertiser, December 15, 1911, p.1.*

[iv] *Interview with JoAnne Rogers House by Gene Glader, March 9, 2002.*

[v] *"Local News," Cook Count News-Herald, August 4, 1927, p.1.*

[vi] *"Grand Opening Advertisement," Cook County News-Herald, August 4, 1927, p. 4.*

[vii] *"Cascade Lodge Open," Cook County News-Herald, June 21, 1928, p. 1.*

[viii] *Interview with JoAnne Rogers House by Gene Glader, March 9, 2002.*

[ix] *"Charles Rogers Weds Wyoming Girl," Cook County News-Herald, March 28, 1929, p. 1.*

[x] *"White Bus Company Advertisement," Cook County News-Herald, January 3, 1924, p. 4.*

[xi] *Populations of Counties by Decennial Census: 1900 to 1990, Compiled and edited by Richard L. Forstall, Population Division, U.S. Bureau of the Census, April 20, 1995.*

[xii] *"Brule Club has Twenty-Six Local Members," Cook County News-Herald, May 9, 1929, p. 1.*

[xiii] *Book 6, Misc., p. 285, Cook County Recorders Office, Grand Marais, MN. E. L. Ogilvie to Morris H. Olson, "Notice of Vendee of Cancellation of Contract Conveyance of Real Property."*

[xiv] *Book 6, Misc., p. 285. Cook County Recorders Office, Grand Marais, MN. E. L. Ogilvie to Morris H. Olson, "Affidavit of Failure to comply with Notice."*

[xv] *Book 6, Misc., p. 285. Cook County Recorders Office, Grand Marais, MN. E. L. Ogilvie to Morris H. Olson, "Affidavit of Failure to comply with Notice."*

[xvi] *"Proof of Claim of Charles E. Rogers," Gowan-Lenning-Brown Co. vs. Cascade Lodge, Inc. District Court, Second Judicial District, Ramsey County, State of Minnesota, July 31, 1935.*

[xvii] *Annual Report, Minnesota Arrowhead Association, 1931, p. 16.*

[xviii] *"North Shore Road To Be Oiled," Cook County News-Herald, March 13, 1930, p. 1.*

[xix] *"Road Worker Killed in Accident Near Cascade," Cook County News-Herald, September 29, 1932, p. 1.*

[xx] *"Preliminary Work on Highway 1 Finished," Cook County News-Herald, September 15, 1932, p. 1.*

[xxi] *Book 5, Mtges. Book 548, Cook County Recorders Office, Grand Marais, MN. Ed. Nunstedt to Cascade Lodge, et al, "Mechanic's Lien", Recorded April 9, 1934.*

[xxii] *"Complaint," Gowan-Lenning-Brown Co. vs. Cascade Lodge, Inc. District Court, Second Judicial District, Ramsey County, State of Minnesota, August 14, 1931.*

[xxiii] *"Complaint" Gowan-Lenning-Brown Co. vs. Cascade Lodge, Inc. District Court, Second Judicial District, Ramsey County, State of Minnesota, January 9, 1932.*

[xxiv] *"Hirmer Named Bank Director," Cook County News-Herald, January 8, 1931, p.1.*

[xxv] *"A. E. Nunstedt Made Director of Local Bank," Cook County News-Herald, January 7, 1932, p. 1.*

[xxvi] *Interview with JoAnne Rogers House, by Gene Glader March 9, 2002.*

[xxvii] *Interview with Edna Seglem Johnson, by Gene Glader on June 15, 2002.*

[xxviii] *Cook County News-Herald, July 14, 1932, p. 4.*

[xxix] *"New Managers of Cascade Lodge," Cook County News-Herald, June 21, 1934, p. 4.*

[xxx] *"Petition," Gowan-Lenning-Brown Co. vs. Cascade Lodge, Inc., District Court, Second Judicial District, Ramsey County, State of Minnesota, January 19, 1935.*

[xxxi] *"Order Permitting Sale of Property," Gowan-Lenning-Brown Co. vs. Cascade Lodge, Inc., District Court, Second Judicial District, Ramsey County, State of Minnesota, January 25, 1935.*

[xxxii] *"Order Permitting Sale of Property," Gowan-Lenning-Brown Co. vs. Cascade Lodge, Inc., District Court, Second Judicial District, Ramsey County, State of Minnesota, January 25, 1935.*

[xxxiii] *"Order," Gowan-Lenning-Brown Co. vs. Cascade Lodge, Inc., District Court, Second Judicial District, Ramsey County, State of Minnesota, January 28, 1936.*

# The Neudahl's Early Years 1935-1938

# Chapter IV

## The Neudahls Arrive with Optimism

Shortly after signing the documents involving the purchase Cascade Lodge on March 14, 1935 Mr. & Mrs. Neudahl arrived at the lodge as new, enthusiastic owners. They had good reason to be optimistic about the future. The country was starting to climb out of the depression, the new highway between Grand Marais and Duluth was finished and they had seen the potential of the lodge by managing the business the previous summer.

**Winter Scene of Lodge, perhaps the winter of 1934-35. The photo is similar to the summer scene in the Neudahl's first brochure.**

## Facilities at the Lodge in Early Neudahl Years

It is not certain how many buildings were on lodge property in 1935. Log cabins 1, 2, & 3 were definitely available as rental units. The fact that Cabin 11 is pictured in the first brochure that the Neudahls printed provides evidence of the use of cabin 11 as a rental unit in 1935.[1] Supporting that possibility is a conversation a lodge guest had with Laurene Glader, in the 1980's. The guest

[1] A copy of the Neudahl's first brochure is included at the end of this chapter.

stated that she and her husband were the first ones to stay in cabin 11 and that the year was 1935. The first brochure only mentions log cabins for overnight accommodations indicating that the guest lodging facilities were limited to the four log cabins in 1935. The brochure makes no mention of rental rooms in the old main lodge.

There may have been one or two additional staff cabins at the time. An early photo taken about 1936 shows a building where cabin 9 is currently located. Perhaps this was where Frank Bissell, a man who worked for the Neudahls for several years, lived during the summers. By 1938, or earlier, there was also a building called cabin 5, which was located where guests park their cars for the current motel.

**Cabin # 5 located on current motel parking area. Cabin may have been built earlier.**
*Circa 1938. Photo Courtesy of Valaine Robinet.*

**Cabin 4 in center, Cabin 5 in upper left and Cabin 10 on the right.** *Courtesy of Valaine Robinet. Circa 1953.*

**A close up view of old cabin 10.** *Circa late thirties.*

Somewhere on the property there was also an icehouse. Most likely it was the building adjacent to the west side of the original main lodge, pictured in the photo below. Such a building was necessary for storing ice blocks in the winter for use during the summer. Note the mention of ice in the advertisement reproduced later in this chapter.

**Original main lodge. Building on the left is probably the icehouse. It may also be a storage building.** *Winter 1936.*

## The Neudahl's Transition into Managing the Lodge

When the Neudahls managed the lodge in 1934 and took over as owners in 1935, Mrs. Neudahl, Elvira and LaVerne were probably the only family members to move to the lodge on a full time basis for the summer. It is possible that Herbert A., the son, also worked at the lodge during the summers of 1934 and 1935. We do know that he joined the Civilian Conservation Corps (CCC) sometime in 1935 and was welcomed to Company #2702 at Cascade State Park on October 18, 1935.[i] It not known which of the existing cabins the Neudahl's lived in when they managed the lodge in 1934. They may have stayed in what is now cabin 11 during the summer of 1934 or some other cabin that may have been built by Charles Rogers. By the summer of 1935 they may have built a staff cabin for themselves to stay in. According to former staff members, Mrs. Neudahl, Elvira and LaVerne stayed in a staff cabin located just west of the old lodge a few summers.

Prior to purchasing the lodge Herbert Neudahl worked for the Twin City Rapid Transit Company, commonly called the Street Car Company. It appears that Herbert kept his job in St. Paul for several years. The consensus among former employees interviewed, was that Mr. Neudahl kept his job in St. Paul until the end of World War II in 1945. Perhaps Mr. Neudahl felt that he had to keep his job in St. Paul for financial reasons, since the resort was small and only a seasonal business for many years. It is reasonable to assume that Mr. Neudahl made many weekend trips to the lodge on his days off during the summer. It is even possible that during the summers, he was able to get some short leaves from his job with the Street Car Company. The assumption that Mr. Neudahl kept his job in St. Paul for a few years is also consistent with a statement by Blake Bishop, a grandson of the Neudahls. He stated that Mrs.

**Dam on Cascade Creek which the Rogers or Neudahls may have built for harvesting ice above the dam. The upper side is now filled with gravel. The bridge in the picture was built in the 1970s.**

Neudahl was the one who discovered the lodge and was the primary person in the family that wanted to buy the lodge.[ii] Mrs. Neudahl was also the person most involved in tourism association activities and the lodge spokesperson at public events over the years. For example it was Mrs. Neudahl who said a few words of appreciation to those who attended a banquet celebrating the

Grand Opening of the new lodge building in 1939.[iii] Additional evidence that Herbert Neudahl kept his job in St. Paul is the record in the local newspaper of many vacations that Mrs. Neudahl, Elvira and LaVerne spent primarily in Hot Springs, Arkansas for a month to six weeks in the winter prior to World War II. These trips were apparently part of the family's effort to help Elvira's paralysis. The absence of Mr. Neudahl's name in the newspaper accounts supports the assumption that his job in St. Paul prevented him from going on these trips.

## The Resort Season

During early years of the Neudahl's ownership, the lodge was essentially open only from some time in late April through Labor Day. Although in 1934, when they were managing the lodge, they promoted dances on Saturday nights until October 20th.[iv] It is very unlikely that they served meals after Labor Day during these early years. Since there were no advertisements for dances in the local newspaper after 1934 it is not known if dances were promoted on a regular basis in September and October in other years. It is assumed that Mrs. Neudahl, Elvira and LaVerne returned to St. Paul each year shortly after Labor Day from 1934 to 1945. There is some evidence that at least Mrs. Neudahl stayed at the lodge or returned for weekends until mid October during this period. Supporting the view that the Neudahls returned to St. Paul each year is a report in the local Cook County newspaper on March 1941 that mentions that "Mr. and Mrs. Herb Neudahl of St. Paul are here on a visit."[v] It should also be noted that there were no winterized buildings at the lodge until 1939. One must assume that LaVerne, their youngest daughter must have gone to elementary school part of each year in both St. Paul and Grand Marais during these years. All the other children, with the possible exception of Elvira, had graduated from high school by 1935 when the Neudahls purchased the lodge.

**The Neudahl Family. Left to right. Herbert A., Herbert, Elvira, LaVerne, Minnie and Harriet.** *Circa 1942. Photo courtesy of Valaine Robinet.*

## The Neudahl Children

The Neudahls had six children: Hazel, born in 1912 died as an infant, Harriet, born in 1914, Herbert August born in 1916, Elvira born in 1919, Kenny born in 1922 and LaVerne, born on December 11, 1931. Kenny, the youngest son, was killed in a tragic automobile accident on July 4th, 1924.[vi] At the time, the Neudahls were visiting a relative in St. Croix Falls, Wisconsin. While there, Elvira, who was five years old and Kenny, who was three years and four months old, were crossing a road and were hit by a car. Kenny and Elvira were taken to the Taylors Falls Hospital where Kenny was pronounced dead shortly after arriving. Elvira was able to leave the hospital shortly after arriving. Her dress had gotten caught on the car and she was dragged on the gravel and bruised and scratched, but was not seriously injured. A few days later, however, she became ill and was diagnosed as having lockjaw. Fortunately she survived, but the lower half of her body became partially and permanently paralyzed. A spinal injection given to her by a doctor may have contributed to her paralysis. This was a great tragedy for the family that affected them emotionally and physically the rest of their lives.

### The Neudahl's First Season as Owners

The Neudahls immediately began remodeling and redecorating the original lodge in the spring of 1935.[vii] This and subsequent events indicate that Mrs. Neudahl and perhaps Elvira and LaVerne moved up to the lodge in late March or early April that first year of ownership. On April 18th they advertised a dance on April 22nd with the following line in the ad, "Reopening of More Fun."[viii] The advertisement seems to refer to the "fun" guests had the previous summer at dances. Two weeks later, on May 2[nd,] they advertised the next dance as a "Grand Opening Dance in the Newly Remodeled and Decorated Cascade Lodge."

# Dance

### Saturday, May 11

## *Cascade Lodge*

FEATURING

## ORIN · TOMLING
## And His High Hatters
### FROM DULUTH

### Beverages on Tap
### Lunches

Admission: 75c per Couple

## Restricted Admittance

The following week another dance was scheduled with "Restricted Admittance."
The nature of the restrictions is not known.

**Dance**

SATURday, May 25

. . .

*Cascade Lodge*

. . .

FEATURING

EARL FRANCES

and His Orchestra

FROM DULUTH

. . .

Beverages on Tap
Lunches

. . .

Coming Soon: Boxing
and Wrestling Matches

The fourth advertisement the Neudahls placed in the local newspaper that year promoted a dance on May 25 and stated that boxing and wrestling matches were coming soon. Whether such matches ever took place is doubtful, because they are never mentioned again. About a month later an advertisement was run on June 27, 1935 promoting horseback riding at the lodge. Apparently the Neudahls arranged for some stable to bring in horses during the summers for about three years. In a 1936 North Shore Directory the phrase "Saddle horses for the Cascade trails," was part of an advertisement for the Lodge. However, in the second lodge brochure, which was probably printed in 1939, it states that horseback riding was available nearby rather than at the lodge.

*Ride Horseback for*

HEALTH      EXERCISE      ENJOYMENT
OVER   CASCADE   TRAILS

---

*A New Feature at*

**Cascade Lodge**

For Reservations Call 2-F-14

CASCADE LODGE. Furnished cabins. Modern
Hot and cold running water. Ice and Fuel. Meals.
Saddle horses for the Cascade trails.

**Advertisement in a 1936 Log and Directory of the North Shore of Superior.**

52

The last advertisement featuring Cascade Lodge in the local paper in 1935 was for a New Years' Eve dance. This dance concluded a regular pattern of dances at the lodge promoted by the Neudahls during the summers of 1934 and 1935. The men from the CCC company located in the park were undoubtedly good customers at the lodge. It is interesting to note that there are no advertisements in the local paper for dances or anything else at the lodge from January 1, 1936 until the Grand Opening of the first section of the new lodge on May 6, 1939, with two exceptions. The exceptions were advertisements for two benefit dances for baseball. One was on April 30th and the other on October 15th of 1938.

PLAN YOUR PARTY NOW

# New Year's Eve

# DANCE!

AND . . CELEBRATION

CASCADE    LODGE

MUSIC   BY

*R h y t h m    R a s c a l s*

NOISEMAKERS:—
-:HATS:-
-:STREAMERS

Fun For All   —   All For Fun
Ring Out The Old Year
Ring In The New Year

*Admission   75c per coup.*

Advertisements in the local paper for dances at various places in the county were very common during the late 1920's, 1930's and 1940's. The absence of advertisements in the *Cook County News-Herald* for dances at Cascade Lodge would seem to indicate that the Neudahls discontinued sponsoring dances; but, just the opposite was the case. Many current local residents have commented about dances at the lodge during this time period. Some older residents can personally remember the dances and some residents recall comments by their parents about the dances at Cascade. It is possible that the dances were so popular that the Neudahls did not need to advertise the dances in the local paper or perhaps they promoted the dances in other ways.

## The Stocking of Trout in the Cascade River

Another possible tourist appeal for guests at the lodge and other fishermen was the stocking of 125,000 small brook trout in the new rearing ponds in the Cascade River in June of 1935. The rearing ponds, which were located about four miles up the river from Lake Superior, where U.S. Forest Road # 157 crosses the river, were constructed in the fall of 1934 by men from the Good Harbor Civilian Conservation Corps (CCC) camp. The announcement of the stocking stated that "These brook trout were hatched from native wild trout eggs from Colorado in the Duluth federal fish hatchery early this spring. They will be fed beef hearts three times a day until fall when they will be turned loose in the Cascade river (sic) to seek their fortune. The object of the rearing ponds is to protect and feed the fish throughout the most critical period of their lives until they are large enough to take care of themselves."[ix] The remains of the ponds are still evident today.

**Remains of brook trout ponds on Cascade River by U.S. Forest Service Road # 157.**

## Hay Fever Haven of America

Another promotional theme for tourism on the North Shore in the 1930's was related to hay fever. In 1935 a statewide organization called the "Hay Fever Haven of America" was formed in Duluth. The intent of this organization was to promote the area from Duluth to the Pigeon River as a "health reserve" for hay fever sufferers.[x] For many years the promotion of the area as a place to experience relief from hay fever was a common reference in the lodge's brochures and area promotional material. To understand the importance of this issue one needs to recall that the thirties and forties was a time before modern air conditioning, air filters and antihistamines which today provide relief for many people who suffer from hay fever.

**Cabins 9, 8, & 7 (left to right) as they appeared in the late 1960's and as they probably looked in the late 1930's.**

**Cabins 6 & 7 (right to left) as they appeared in the late 1960's and as they probably looked in the late 1930's.**

## Additional Cabins Built

With the growth of tourism in the area the Neudahl's began expanding their business. Cabins 6, 7, 8 and 9 were most likely all built prior to the building of the new lodge in 1939. It is possible that one or more of the units was built in 1940 or 1941, but it is almost certain that they were all there prior to World War II. It appears that the Neudahls had a total of ten or eleven cabins for guests by about 1940. In addition to the cabins pictured above there were two small staff cabins at the top of the hill behind cabin 6 and a vertical log storage building located a bit further up the driveway. The storage building is still there as of this writing and is in the process of being restored for historical purposes.

None of the cabins were winterized, but at least some of them had either a cooking stove or propane or kerosene heaters for warmth during early spring and fall nights. Water for the cabins came from the artesian wells with the pipes being either above ground or buried just a few inches under the surface. These pipes definitely had to be drained before winter.

## Come to Cascade Lodge
## In Cascade State Park
### —for your vacation

ONE OF THE EIGHT CASCADE WATERFALLS
FOUR OF WHICH MAY BE SEEN FROM ONE POSITION

**RESERVATIONS ARE NOW BEING MADE**

### HOW TO GET THERE

By train to Duluth and Bus to Grand Marais.
By Bus to Duluth, change to Bus for Grand Marais.
By Auto over U. S. Highway No. 61.

Rates—American Plan

| | |
|---|---|
| Per Day . . . . . | $ 3.50 to $ 4.50 |
| Per Week . . . . . | $21.00 to $28.00 |
| One-half rates for children under 12. | |
| Housekeeping Cabins . . $15.00 to $30.00 per week | |

## CASCADE LODGE

Telephone 10 R 2     GRAND MARAIS, MINNESOTA
Midway Between Duluth and Port Arthur

H. NEUDAHL, Prop.

**CASCADE LODGE**

CASCADE STATE PARK
Minnesota's Finest Rustic Resort
On The Great North Shore
Of Lake Superior

On Minn. Highway No. 1—U. S. Highway No. 61
10½ Miles Southwest of Grand Marais, Minn.

**The back and front panels of the Neudahl's first brochure.** *Circa 1935.*

57

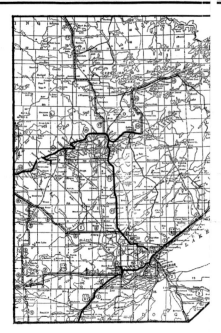

### Mileage Table to Cascade Lodge

| | |
|---|---|
| From Duluth . . . . . . . | 100 Miles |
| " Port Arthur . . . . . | 100 " |
| " Twin Cities . . . . . | 256 " |
| " Ely . . . . . . . | 109 " |
| " Fargo . . . . . . . | 382 " |
| " Milwaukee . . . . . . | 541 " |
| " Sioux City . . . . . . | 540 " |

Ten and One-half Miles Southwest of
Grand Marais

## A Wonderful Place to Play and to Rest

PART OF THE DINING ROOM IN THE MAIN LODGE

FISHING—Lake and brook trout in all nearby lakes and streams. Good sport whipping the fly on Cascade River and others.

HIKING—Numerous trails thru Cascade Park and old logging roads through a wilderness country of beautiful scenery. Glorious days in woods and along streams.

KODAKING—Wonderful views and opportunities for pictures of game and wild life.

MOTORING—On broad, smooth macadamized highways over the longest stretch of blue water highway in the world and on motor trails through virgin forests.

HUNTING—Bear, deer and an abundance of small game.

RESTING—A haven for hay fever sufferers. Cool nights and glorious days—with always a cool breeze from the lake—in the fragrant piney air of the north woods.

BOATING—Motor boating on Superior or one of many nearby lakes—wonderful canoe trips on northern lakes.

**First inside fold of the Neudahl's first brochure.** *Circa 1935.*

"A
*Friendly Spot
in the Arrowhead"*

HERE on America's most scenic highway, in the land of big game, big fish, and amidst the scenic grandeur of Cascade State Park, is located CASCADE LODGE, a new, modern, comfortable resort, with a big rustic log lodge and dining room, and log cabin sleeping accommodations. Whether you want to be alone or mingle with other congenial vacationists—here is the ideal spot—in the friendly atmosphere and beautiful surroundings of this wilderness resort of luxury and good comradeship.

Exactly halfway between Duluth and Port Arthur, on the famous North Shore Road, this resort in the center of the north country—"The Playground of the World," is situated on the side of a bluff overlooking Lake Superior. The highway passes immediately in front of the resort and within fifty feet of the rocky shore line.

This is one of the finest settings for a resort that can be imagined—a beautiful place of primeval wilderness on the shores of Lake Superior and beside the beautiful Cascade River, which winds its way thun-

derously through Cascade Park. The entire resort is backed up by a dense forest of pine, fir and birch. The changes that have been made in this rugged setting are simple and few, and only those essential to the complete comfort and convenience of visitors to Cascade Lodge and Cascade Park. The rugged beauty of this famous North Country has remained unspoiled. It is an ideal combination of natural beauty and comparative detachment from the outer world, and the necessary conveniences to whole-hearted enjoyment of its beauties and of its opportunities for play and rest.

The Main Lodge is a beautiful log structure with a wide veranda across the front. Inside, at each end, are enormous stone fireplaces, comfortable davenports, chairs, desks, piano and good books on the stone mantlepiece. Here in the Lodge, also, is the beautiful dining room, where the meals served are already famous for their excellence. The Lodge is about twenty feet above the level of the lake, and in back of it the wooded, rocky bluff rises to a height of one hundred feet above the lake level.

ONE OF THE CABINS

The log cabins, the finest that can be built, extend in two rows to one side and back up the bluff among the pines, and on either side of the mountain stream that tumbles down its rocky course to the lake. A rustic log bridge leads across the stream to the second row of cabins.

These cabins—all as secluded and delightfully located as a private summer home—are equipped with every convenience. Each has a screened-in porch, bath room, hot and cold running water, and electric lights.

**Second inside fold of the Neudahl's first brochure.** *Circa 1935.*

The above brochure is the first one produced by the Neudahls. It is not known if this brochure was available in the spring of 1935, but it clearly served the period from 1935 through 1938. Some 1930 era terms used in the brochure are " Kodaking," "Motoring," and "Macadamized highways." On the inside of the brochure is a picture of what today is called Cabin 11. It is located behind the current restaurant and guests could cross a little footbridge to get to it. In the picture a chimney is located at the north end of the cabin. In 1946 a stone fireplace was added to the south end of the cabin and the original chimney removed.

The rates in 1938 for a housekeeping cabin or sleeping cabin were $2.00 and up per day. For American Plan guests the rate was $3.50 per day and up or $21.00 per week and up. Being on the American Plan meant lodging and three meals a day were included. These prices were comparable to those at other resorts in the area. A few resorts started at $4.00 per day for American Plan guests and one resort had cabins advertised for as low as $1.00 per day. The following advertisement was in the 1938 Minnesota Arrowhead Association Hotel and Resort Directory.

## CASCADE LODGE

One hundred miles north of Duluth. Cascade State Park, overlooking Lake Superior. Hot and cold running water, showers, electricity. Central dining room. Housekeeping and sleeping cabins, $2 up. American Plan, $3.50 day, up; $21 week, up. Fine fishing in nearby lakes and streams. A haven for hay fever sufferers. H. Neudahl, Prop. Address—Grand Marais, Minnesota.

The fact that housekeeping cabins were mentioned in the above advertisement suggests that cabins 6 or 7 or 10 or all three of the cabins, were built by 1938. These were the cabins with kitchens. A photo, presumably taken in 1939, which shows cabin 6, supports the theory that the above advertisement is referring to at least cabin 6. It does not appear that log cabins 1, 2, and 3 ever had kitchens. Cabin 11 probably did have a kitchen prior to 1946.

### Electricity Becomes Available

When electricity was first available at the lodge is not certain. The first advertisement mentioning the availability of electricity at the lodge was in the 1938 Minnesota Arrowhead Association Directory. However, the first brochure distributed by the Neudahls, which may have been printed as early as 1935, mentions that the log cabins had electricity for lights. Because of these references it must be concluded that the lodge had an electric generator at least by 1938 if not sooner. As was pointed out in Chapter II, there is some evidence that cabins 1, 2, 3 and 11 had electricity for lights as early as 1923.

In the spring of 1937 a cooperative was formed in Cook County for the purpose of bringing electricity to the shore from Naniboujou Lodge to Schroeder. The plan was to become part of the federal government rural electrification program. A preliminary survey showed that between Grand Marais and Schroeder 153 users would sign up.[xi] Although the effort was ultimately successful, electricity from outside sources did not arrive at Cascade Lodge prior to November 17, 1941.[2]

## A New Main Lodge is Planned

By the end of the 1938 tourist season the Neudahls had made a big decision. They had decided to tear down the original log lodge and build a hotel type main lodge. They announced in October of 1938 that the new structure would have ten guest rooms, steam heat, a fireplace, and a recreation room. They also planned to build a tennis court on the site of the original lodge.[xii] The tennis court was never built. Some people have said that the original main lodge burned down, but an article in the local paper indicates that the lodge was torn down. What may have transpired is that after some of the building was torn down the Neudahls may have burned some of the old logs and boards on the site.

The tearing down of the original main lodge marked the end of an era at Cascade. The rustic, old lodge had been the focal point of guest services for 12 years and the resort was rebuilding to meet the expectation and needs of guests during a new era.

---

[2] November 13, 1947 the Lutsen Light & Power Co. ran an advertisement in the Cook County News-Herald celebrating its seventh anniversary. The add stated that on November 17, 1941 power was turned on to 21 customers within four miles of the plant. Cascade Lodge was beyond this distance and did not receive power on that date.

[i] *The Jaybird, CCC Company #2702, Cascade State Park, Lutsen, Minnesota, Vol. 2 Number 3, October 18, 1935, p. 1.*

[ii] *Interview with Blake Bishop by Gene Glader at Cascade Lodge, June 1997.*

[iii] *"Cascade Lodge Has Grand Opening," <u>Cook County News-Herald</u>, May 11, 1939, p.1.*

[iv] *Farewell Dance Advertisement, <u>Cook County News-Herald</u>, October 18, p. 2.*

[v] *"Local News," <u>Cook County News-Herald</u>, March 13, 1941, p. 1.*

[vi] *"CHILDREN RUN DOWN IN INTERSTATE PARK, "<u>The Standard Press</u>, St. Croix Falls, Wisconsin, July 10, 1924, p. 1.*

[vii] *"Cascade Lodge Changes Hands," <u>Cook County News-Herald</u>, March 28, 1935, p.1.*

[viii] *Advertisement, <u>Cook County News-Herald</u>, April 18, 1935, p. 3.*

[ix] *"Brook Trout Are Put in Cascade," <u>Cook County News-Herald</u>, June 20, 1935, p. 1.*

[x] *"Hay Fever Haven to Be Advertised," <u>Cook County News-Herald</u>, March 7, 1935, p. 4.*

[vi] *"Plans Made for Electrification of Shore; G.M. to Schroeder," <u>Cook County News-Herald</u>, April 15, 1937, p.1.*

[xii] *"New Hotel to Replace Cascade Lodge," <u>Cook County News-Herald</u>, October 27, 1938, p. 1.*

# Cascade River State Park History

## Chapter V

### The Connection between the Lodge and the Park

The history of Cascade Lodge is intimately connected to the Cascade River, the surrounding area and the history of Cascade River State Park. The very location of the lodge undoubtedly was selected due to the beauty and proximity of the river. Chapter I pointed out that the original parcel of land from which the lodge acreage was sold, included land from just west of the lodge, the river frontage and the entire current park campground.

### The Purchase of the Park Land

After completing the improvements to Highway 61 in 1933, the Minnesota Highway Department purchased about 2,300 acres of land near the mouth of the Cascade River, stretching along the highway for several miles from the vicinity of Spruce Creek west of Cascade Lodge to at least Highway 7 east of the lodge. A key factor in the emergence of Cascade River State Park was the fact that by 1922, Fred D. McMillen had become the owner of most of the land that was to become the park.

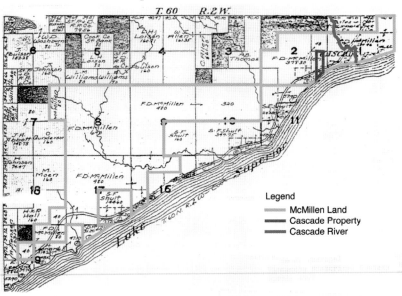

**Land owned by Fred D. McMillen in 1934 has his name in the section. The numbers in the squares are section numbers.**

Step one in the process of selling the land to the State of Minnesota involved Fred D. McMillen selling the future park land that he owned in sections 1, 2, 6, 10, and 16 to the Ogema Land & Abstract Company on March 14, 1934. Then the Ogema Land & Abstract Company sold the land to the state between March 20, 1934 and December 31, 1934. It appears that the Ogema Land and Abstract Company was assisting the Highway Department in obtaining the land it desired. A small parcel of land about 100 feet wide, located east of the lodge and between the lake and the highway was owned by Frank Bissell and he sold it to the State of Minnesota on December 6, 1935. Frank was an employee at the lodge for many years during the thirties and forties. The combined land became the largest wayside park of the Minnesota Highway Department. At that time it was known as Cascade Wayside.[i] It was intended that the wayside would eventually be turned over to the Department of Conservation's State Park Division.[ii] This department was the forerunner of the current Department of Natural Resources. The transfer of the Cascade Wayside, except for land in the highway right-of-way, to the State Parks Division of the Minnesota Department of Conservation took place in 1957 by an act of the legislature. It was at this time that the Cascade Wayside was officially designated as Cascade River State Park.

## The Cascade Overlook

The focal point of the land purchased in 1934 was a stretch approximately 550 feet long at the mouth of the river that was to become known as the Cascade River Overlook. In 1932 the Highway Department built a new bridge over the river at this location and actually altered the directional flow of the river into Lake Superior. The new reinforced concrete, arched bridge is approximately 350 feet east of the location of the 1916 bridge. The first water falls are approximately 300 feet up the river from the highway.

**Bridge over Cascade River Built in 1932. Note the stone wall built by CCC personnel in 1934 & 1935.** *Photo circa 1955.*

## The Spruce Creek CCC Camp

The development of the Cascade River Wayside, Cascade River Overlook and shoulders of Highway 61 within the 2,300 acre wayside and what is today the camping area within the park, all received a big boast from the Civilian Conservation Corps program. The CCC was a major federal program, which employed thousands of unemployed young men during the depression to work on projects around the country. On July 24, 1934 a CCC camp began in what is today called the Cascade River State Park. The CCC camp… "was named the Spruce Creek CCC Camp, rather than the 'Cascade River Camp,' because another CCC camp known as the Cascade River Camp had already been established in 1933 by the U.S. Forest Service several miles to the north."[iii] The new camp was officially called Spruce Creek CCC Camp Company 2702. It was also initially number DSP–5 and later SP-13. DSP stood for Division of State Parks and SP stood for State Park.

There were twelve other CCC camps in Cook County. From 1933 to 1940 thousands of men came to Cook County and worked on various Civilian Conservation Corps (CCC) projects. The Spruce Creek Camp was under the jurisdiction of the National Park Service, the Minnesota Parks Division of the State Department of Conservation and the U.S. Army. The work done by the camp enrollees was considered a success and stimulated the establishments of three other camps under the sponsorship of the Minnesota Highway Department in other areas of the state.

**Sign for Spruce Creek Camp near Cascade River.** *Photo courtesy of CCC Archives.*

The Spruce Creek camp began with about 200 men living in temporary quarters at the vacated Caribou Lake CCC Camp which was located about eight miles west of the Cascade River. Each day the men were transported to the Cascade site to work. At first some of the men worked on the construction of the barracks, dining hall, recreation building and garages while other men began working on projects related to the basic purpose of the camp. "By the end of September, the CCC had developed 6,000' of walking trails in the Cascade Wayside, built a service road into the CCC camp site, planted [grass on] 1.6 miles of highway slopes, landscaped ledges, and had begun to build the overlook wall."[iv] The men moved into the ten new barracks on October 16, 1934. Two days later *THE JAYBIRD*, the camp's mimeographed newspaper noted that four new men, including Herbert Neudahl, were welcomed into the camp.[v] Herbert was the son of Mr. & Mrs. Herbert Neudahl the owners of Cascade Lodge.

The site of the camp was located in the general area of the current Cascade River State Park campground. The ten barracks which were constructed were originally intended to be used as tourist cabins when the site was turned over to the State Parks Division.

**Viewing area frequently referred to as "Five Falls" on the Cascade River from the walking bridge.**

By November the company had built 165 feet of the overlook wall by the Cascade River. To continue the work throughout the winter months they built a shelter over the wall in the fall and heated the work area in the winter. By the end of May, 1935 the wall was basically finished. In the spring of 1935 the men constructed a footbridge over the river a few hundred feet up the river from the first waterfall. It is a very scenic spot.

## Building the Bridge over Cascade Creek

Of particular interest to Cascade Lodge was the replacing of an old concrete culvert type bridge over the creek east of the main lodge driveway. In its place a new concrete and stone bridge was constructed during the summer of 1935.[vi] In the CCC documents the creek is labeled Babineau Creek, but the creek has been called Cascade Creek for at least thirty-five years. The bridge, which is primarily on lodge property, was part of a trail going west along the shore.[1] At the time the creek bridge was built, the current Cascade Restaurant building did not exist. At this time the gasoline pump at the lodge was west of the creek. It is visible in a photo in chapter VI.

**Original bridge over Cascade Creek. Note hill where current restaurant is located and red crown gasoline sign in left side of picture.** *Circa 1934. Photo from CCC archives.*

---

[1] The footbridge is located primarily outside highway department right-of-away which includes land up to fifty feet from the center line of the highway.

**Close up view of original bridge across the Cascade Creek. Note cabins 1 and 2 in the background.**

**Construction of bridge over Cascade Creek. Note old bridge and hand rails and sign for Red Crown gasoline. 1935.** *Photo courtesy of Marilyn Starr who's father worked on the bridge.*

**69**

Finished bridge over Cascade Creek. The location is a few feet west of the original bridge. At this time the gasoline pump was west of the creek. It is visible in a photo in chapter II. *1935.*

## Camp Entertainment

For entertainment at the camp there was a recreation building with ping pong, pool tables and a canteen. Dances were also held in the building. In addition, the men frequently walked to Cascade Lodge or to the Rainbow Inn for food, beer and dancing. The Rainbow Inn was located on the Cascade Beach Road near the intersection with Highways 61. The visits by the men from the CCC camp were undoubtedly good business for both establishments. Both the Rainbow Inn and Cascade Lodge ran advertisements in the camp newspaper.

Advertisements in October 30, 1935 JAYBIRD.

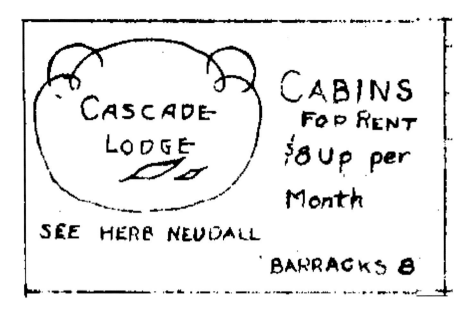

Advertisement in Nov. 11, 1935 CCC JAYBIRD. Herb Neudahl must have been booking some off-season use of cabins from his barrack. Perhaps for the hunting season. The cabins were not winterized.

## The Closing of the CCC Camp
## and Increase in Visitors to the Park

The CCC camp at the Cascade Wayside Park closed in 1937. In contrast to the originally planned use of the barracks, all the buildings were torn down except for the mess hall and two barracks which were used for a while by the highway department.

What began as a wayside highway stop and overlook has grown in popularity over the years. Visitor attendance data at the park not only documents the growing popularity of the park as a destination; it also parallels the overall growth of tourism on the North Shore. The visitor attendance trends at the park are as follows: day use visitors numbered just over 7,000 in 1958 and jumped to approximately 100,000 in 1979.[vii] In 1990 the reported number of day user visits to the park was 159,343[viii] and in 2000 there were 128,995.[ix] These numbers aren't absolute because they are based on some hard data and some estimates by different managers. There has been some fluctuation in the number of day user visits at the park due to various circumstances, such as the economy and weather, but the overall trend is accurate. The number of overnight campers using the park in the year 2000 was 12,792.[x]

## The Weather at Cascade

Information regarding the weather which was reported in a park document is of interest to guests at the park as well as at the lodge. The document reports as follows:

"Because of the influence of Lake Superior, Cascade River State Park tends to be cooler in the summer and warmer in the winter than inland areas of the state.

"The climate of Cascade is ideal for recreation throughout the year. The moderating effect of Lake Superior tends to extend the normal summer recreation season well into the fall, making the area ideal for picnicking, hiking, and camping. Winter recreation conditions are also ideal. The season is long and mild and has abundant snowfall. In contrast to the metropolitan area [Minneapolis & St. Paul] which has an average of 166 days a year below freezing, the Cascade area only has 144 days below freezing. There is usually a suitable snow cover for winter sports from the beginning of December until the middle of April."[xi]

**Postcard photo of Cascade River flowing under the 1932 bridge.**
*Circa 1950's. Photo by Gallagher's Studio.*

## The Complimentary Relationship
## between the Lodge and the Park

As is clearly evident, the lodge and the park share a special location on the shore of Lake Superior. Over the years the lodge and the park have enjoyed a great relationship and have complimented each other's facilities. The most obvious complimentary facilities are the camping facilities provided by the park and the lodging and restaurant facilities provided by the lodge. The various owners of the lodge and the managers of the park have also shared a vision to preserve the area for future generations. The sharing of hiking and ski trails, and naturalist programs are just a few examples of how these entities have partnered together. The Superior National Forest has also been a great partner in the development and sharing of trails. The relationship between Cascade Lodge, Cascade River State Park and the Superior National Forest has truly been a wonderful example of private enterprise, and state and federal governmental agencies working together. Obviously, there is much more to the history of Cascade River State Park that is beyond the scope and relevance of a book on the history of Cascade Lodge. However, some information about the park is necessary for an understanding of the development of Cascade Lodge.

[i] *MNDOT Historic Roadside Development Structures Inventory, Reference No. CK-UOG-044 CS 1602 Cascade River Overlook, by Susan Granger and Scott Kelly of Gemini Research, August 9, 1999, p. 9.*

[ii] *MNDOT Historic Roadside Development Structures Inventory, Reference No. CK-UOG-044 CS 1602 Cascade River Overlook, by Susan Granger and Scott Kelly of Gemini Research, August 9, 1999, p. 9.*

[iii] *MNDOT Historic Roadside Development Structures Inventory, Reference No. CK-UOG-044 CS 1602 Cascade River Overlook, by Susan Granger and Scott Kelly of Gemini Research, August 9, 1999, p. 6.*

[iv] *MNDOT Historic Roadside Development Structures Inventory, Reference No. CK-UOG-044 CS 1602 Cascade River Overlook, by Susan Granger and Scott Kelly of Gemini Research, August 9, 1999, p. 6.*

[v] *CCC Company # 2702, ed., THE JAYBIRD, October 18, 1935, p.1.*

[vi] *"Narrative Report, April 1 to October 1, 1935," Spruce Creek DSP#5, Lutsen, MN, Division of State Parks, National Park Service, Department of Interior, Washington, D.C.*

[vii] *"A Summary of the Cascade River State Park Management Plan," Minnesota Department of natural Resources, Office of Planning, St. Paul, MN, December 1981, p. 5.*

[viii] *"Cascade River State Park 1990 Annual Activity Report", Department of Natural Resources, St. Paul, MN, 1990, p. 1.*

[ix] *"Cascade River State Park Management Plan," Department of Natural Resources, St. Paul, MN, 2003, p. 12.*

[x] *"Cascade River State Park Management Plan," Department of Natural Resources, St. Paul, MN, 2003, p. 12.*

[xi] *Arthur Sidner, Director, State Planning Agency, "Final Review of Cascade River Recreational) State Park Management Plan," Minnesota State Planning Agency, St. Paul, MN June 19, 1981, p. 22.*

# The New Lodge 1939

## Chapter VI

### The New Main Lodge

The new lodge was completed as scheduled by the spring of 1939. A Grand Opening Banquet was held on May 6, 1939 with members of the Grand Marais Commercial Club in attendance.[i] The new lodge was built on the lakeside of the driveway that led to the old lodge. A children's play area currently occupies the site of the original lodge. The mature row of spruce trees by the play area are the same little trees that stood in front of the original lodge some 75 years ago.

Cascade Lodge, Grand Marais, Minn.

**Postcard of the new lodge. On the address side of the card Mrs. H. Neudahl was listed as the proprietor.** *Circa 1939.*

The new lodge was designed for ten guest rooms. Because of various remodeling projects in the lodge over the years, the location and layout of the original rooms is not exactly clear. One possibility is that there were ten rooms on the second floor of the lodge: three rooms with bathrooms and seven with only a sink or lavatory as it was called then. The 1949 rate sheet reproduced at the end of this chapter could be interpreted to support this arrangement. There were also two public bathrooms on the second floor with tub/showers for guests without a toilet and bath facilities in their rooms.

Another possibility is that there were nine rooms on the second floor and one on the first floor which the Neudahls used. With this arrangement, all the rooms in the 1939 lodge, except two, had full baths. This was the arrangement when the Neudahls sold the lodge in 1969. The current living room area was the dining room, and the kitchen was part of what are now rooms 101 and 103. On the first floor there was also a guest living room with a fireplace, a lobby and a room adjacent to the lobby that was a combination of office and bedroom space for the Neudahl family. In the basement was a recreation room and additional public bathrooms.

The rocks for the patio and chimney at the new main lodge came from the chimneys of CCC buildings in the Cascade Wayside Park and from rock along the highway between the lodge and the park campground. After the Spruce Creek CCC Camp closed in 1937, and most of the buildings were torn down, the fireplaces remained and the rocks used to construct the fireplaces became available to whoever wanted them. Mr. Neudahl apparently capitalized on the

**New lodge with a sign on front lawn. Note cabin with porch in background and small trees on lawn.** *Summer 1939. Photo by Milford J. Humphrey.*

availability of the rocks and used them in building the new main lodge. He probably collected a sufficient supply of rocks at the time to later use on the restaurant building and the west wing addition to the main lodge.[ii]

The cabin in the background, in the picture opposite, was probably built during the Neudahl's first years at the lodge. This appears to have been a staff cabin and is very similar to the staff cabin currently located next to the old garage by the main lodge. The cabin appears to have a porch in the picture. If that is the case, the porch must have been removed prior to the cabin being moved to its current location. A garage and another staff cabin were located behind the lodge. These buildings were most likely built in the late thirties or early forties.

**New lodge with gas pump on the left side of driveway. The addition to rooms 101 and 103 did not exist. Note driveway toward cabin 11.**
*Circa 1939. Photo by Milford .J. Humphrey.*

**Cabin 11 with seven deer on the bridge on Nov. 16, 1940. Ben Klima hunting party.** *Photo courtesy of Valinda Littfin, granddaughter of Ben Klima.*

## Deer Hunting Seasons

During the thirties and forties deer were in great abundance in the area and it became a popular destination for deer hunters. The habitat in the area was conducive to the growth and reproduction of deer because the forest was still young as the result of logging during the early part of the century and the forest fires during the twenties.

According to Dorothy Gunderson, the daughter of Ben Klima, her father stayed in cabin 11 and hunted deer in the area for several years in the late thirties and forties. Other photos indicate that he came to the lodge with six or seven other men from the Silver Lake and Hutchinson, Minnesota area. At this time none of the cabins were winterized, which means they had no running water, no storm windows and no insulation to keep the heat in and the cold out during deer season in November. This does not appear to have been a problem for the hunters.

During this period the main tourist season ended with Labor Day with perhaps some business for a few weeks in September and October. It is very likely that Frank Bissell, a local employee of the Neudahls, who lived at the lodge in the summer and in the area in the winter, checked the men in and out during deer hunting season. It is also possible that one of the Neudahls came up to the lodge from St. Paul during hunting season and other occasions during the late fall and winter months.

**Cabin 11 prior to the addition of a stone fireplace on south end.**
*Circa 1941. Photo by Milford J. Humphrey.*

## World War II Years

During the summers of 1939 through 1941 tourism continued to expand on the North Shore and Cascade Lodge, with its new main lodge, began attracting more guests. An interruption in the expansion, however, came during the war years of 1942 through 1945. These were challenging times for resorts throughout the country. Although the United States was at war in 1942, civilians were encouraged to participate in recreational activities on their days off and to take vacations for their health and morale. In an effort to promote this concept, Harold L. Ickes, Secretary of the Interior emphasized in a statement that "America should profit by the experience of warring nations who learned in war that too long hours at high pressure work resulted in decreased production."[iii] Even the Neudahls, namely Mrs. Neudahl, Elvira and LaVerne spent about four weeks during March and February of 1942 vacationing in Florida and visiting twelve states[iv] before gas rationing began.

By June 1942 tourism leaders were devising strategies as to how to deal with the impending threat of gas rationing. Part of this strategy was to convince the national leaders in Washington, D.C. to postpone the implementation of gas rationing until after September 1, 1942.[v] This effort must have had some influence because congress did not institute gas rationing until November of 1942.[vi] However, a 40 miles per hour speed limit was begun in June of 1942.[vii] The lower speed limit probably kept people in the midwest from taking long trips to the mountain states and to the Pacific and Atlantic states. This view is in line with a report by the Grand Marais Chamber of Commerce in June of 1942, which stated that "Most of the inquiries are from Minnesota."[viii] Tourism on the North Shore seems to have held fairly steady during the summer of 1942. In fact 1942 may have been the real beginning of fall tourist business on the North Shore. E. F. Lindquist, Secretary of the Grand Marais Chamber of Commerce commented as follows about the fall business on September 3, 1942.

"In former years the feeling among us on the North Shore was that the tourism season would end by Labor Day. However, this year it appears somewhat different, that is, if we are to judge by the amount of inquiries in for September and October vacations.

"I have tried to find the cause for this unusual turn, and in making inquiries from such parties found the following:

" ' We may not have either gas or tires next year, so we are taking our vacation now.'

" 'With the constant demand for defense workers, and with the continued effort of such projects to keep everybody busy, we may not get time off next year for our vacation, so we are coming this fall.'

"The North Shore has a great deal to offer during the months of September and October in its beautiful fall coloring and many of the flowers still in full bloom."[ix]

Although no records are available, it seems safe to assume that Cascade Lodge benefited from some of this fall business. Due to the War the summer of 1942 was most likely the last good year of business for Cascade Lodge and other resorts until 1946.

As the war continued the summers of 1943, 1944 and 1945 were difficult for resorts. As early as June of 1942 resorts were encouraged by the local Chamber of Commerce to refrain from elaborate expansions, to not over advertise and to keep their overhead down.[x] Because of the war there were probably no buildings added or major improvements to the Cascade Lodge property from 1942 until Japan surrendered on August 15, 1945.

The rationing of gas, tires, coffee and sugar and the inability to purchase many products certainly created challenges for people in the hospitality business. An example of the difficulties caused by various shortages is a situation confronted by Cherry's Bakery in Grand Marais as late as August 29, 1946. It had to close a few days because its sugar allotment had run out.[xi] During these years traveling to the lodge by bus was promoted as an alternative mode of transportation. Guests could get off and be picked up right at the lodge driveway. This option is still available today.

During the prohibition years of 1920 to 1933 it was illegal to manufacture, sell or transport alcoholic beverages in the United States. In Cook County it remained difficult to obtain a license to sell liquor for several additional years. However, it was legal to sell beer in the county. Mrs. Neudahl is reported to have had her own way of dealing with the lack of a license to sell liquor. According to a young lady who was a waitress and housekeeper at the lodge for a few weeks during the summer of 1942, Mrs. Neudahl served liquor in the lodge and hid a supply of it in the sawdust in the icehouse. The employee remembers how either Frank Bissell, the maintenance man, or one of the waitresses would have to go out and get the liquor in the icehouse when Mrs. Neudahl needed some for guests in the lodge.[xii]

Even though the business of operating the lodge may have been difficult during the war years the Neudahls kept the lodge open during the summers. Evidence of this is the fact that the Junior-Senior Banquet for the Cook County High School was held at Cascade Lodge in 1943[xiii] and the report in the local newspaper in August 1944 that Mrs. Harold Stassen, the wife of the former Governor of Minnesota, and her son were vacationing at the lodge while Mr. Stassen was in the service of his country.[xiv] Over the years Mr. & Mrs. Stassen stayed at the lodge many times including a visit in the 1980's.

When the War ended in August of 1945 the U.S. began the process of converting to a peacetime economy. A part of this process was the conversion of automobile factories from manufacturing military vehicles to the manufacturing of civilian cars and trucks. This met a great pent up need for cars and trucks and contributed to the growth in the resort business and to the overall economy. Americans had not been able to buy new cars since 1941 and they were anxious to hit the roads.

GRAND
OPENING
DANCE
IN THE NEW
**Cascade**
**I n n**
Music by
VERNIE, MARVEL AND FOSTER
**Saturday**
**JUNE 14**

## The Addition of the Coffee Shop

After WW II the Neudahls decided to increase the facilities at the lodge again. The first major project was the building of the Coffee Shop/gas station which is the current restaurant building. The building was most likely started in 1946, and we know it was finished in the spring of 1947, because a "Grand Opening Dance" was held in the building on June 14, 1947.[xv] The building was called the Cascade Inn in the June 14th advertisement and again in an advertisement for a July 4th dance.[xvi] How long the term "Cascade Inn" was used is not clear. It probably was used for only a few months. The building in reality was a combination coffee shop, bar, gift shop, gas station and dance hall. The main dining room remained in the main lodge. At about the same time that the coffee shop/gas station was being built cabin 11 was remodeled. A major part of the remodeling was the addition of a stone fireplace on the south end of the cabin.

PLAN TO SPEND THE EVE-
NING OF

# JULY FOURTH
# DANCING

—AT—

THE NEW CASCADE INN

Music By

VERNIE, MARVEL and

FOSTER

**Cabin 11 remodeled with a stone fireplace.** *Circa 1946. Photo by Milford J. Humphrey.*

**New gas station and coffee shop. Sign in front is a Fitgers beer sign. The top of the new stone fireplace for cabin 11 can be seen to the right and back of the coffee shop building.** *Circa 1947. Photo by Milford J. Humphrey.*

## Alpine Skiing Facilities Developed in Cook County

During the post War era skiing emerged in Cook County as a winter activity. From very humble beginnings skiing would develop into a major winter activity attracting many guests to Cascade Lodge and other area resorts. The first recorded ski meet in the area was in late February, 1947. The event was sponsored by Clarence Krotz, the owner of Skyport Lodge on Devil's Track Lake. The meet was on Maple Hill and consisted of some type of run with obstacles and a jump.[xvii] A year and ten months later, in December 1948 Lutsen Resort opened the Lutsen Resort Ski Area, and a group of men from Grand Marais opened the Sawtooth Mountain Ski Slide on the hill behind the town.[xviii] With the opening of the Lusten Ski Area the Nelsons of Lutsen Resort asked for help in housing visiting skiers to the area.[xix] The development of the two ski areas clearly marked the beginning of a new era of winter tourism along the North Shore and in Grand Marais. The Neudahls were living at the lodge on a year-round basis at this time, except for their winter vacations for a few weeks each year to either Arkansas or Florida. Consequently, the Lodge with its ten rooms must have benefited immediately from the ski hill developments, even if the lodge was closed for part of the winter while the Neudahls were on vacation.

## Roller Skating Rink Two Miles Away

A year after the opening of the two ski areas, Mr. and Mrs. E. W. Melquist opened a roller skating rink in early December 1949. The rink was located at the corner of highways 61 and 7 immediately behind what is now called the Cascade House.[xx] The rink was only two miles from the lodge and certainly added another optional activity for guests. The rink closed in the late fifties. Earlier, from about 1938 through 1941, there was a roller skating rink at the Pike Lake Resort, which is located about five miles north of the lodge, but about eleven miles by road.

## The Coffee Shop/Bar/Gas Station

On May 21, 1949 the local high school Prom and Banquet was held at Cascade Lodge. The banquet was held in the dining room of the main lodge (shown below) and the dance in the coffee shop building pictured opposite. That same month LaVerne Neudahl graduated as the valedictorian of her senior class from the local high school.

**Inside view of dining room in the mail lodge.** *Circa 1940's. Photo by Milford J. Humphrey*

**85**

**Marilyn Mattson Nyquist , a summer employee pumping gas. Note air hose on ground that rang a bell so girls would know someone wanted gas. Summer 1949.** *Photo courtesy of Marilyn Mattson Nyquist.*

In the spring of 1949 Marilyn Mattson, who grew up in Duluth, responded to an advertisement for help by the Neudahls in the Duluth paper. She was hired. Her job was to pump gas, cook, wait tables in the coffee shop and work as a clerk in the gift shop. She recalls that Mrs. Neudahl would open the cafe in the morning and someone would bring the soup of the day down from the main dining room kitchen. Then at noon Mrs. Neudahl would bring down the noon special for the coffee shop from the lodge kitchen. The menu at the cafe was mainly hamburgers, hot dogs, soup and beverages. The girls were not allowed to call up to the lodge for help unless there were more than three cars at the cafe. In the evenings Mrs. Neudahl worked at the cafe and Marilyn and the other young girls were not allowed to go to the building after 7 p.m.[1] This rule apparently had something to do with the type of adult clientele that came on some nights and the drinking that took place in the evenings.

## Cascade Lodge and Cabins

### RATE SHEET — 1949 SEASON

#### MAIN LODGE

| Description of Room | Number of Persons | American Plan Including Meals | |
|---|---|---|---|
| | | Daily | Weekly |
| Twin beds, private bath, lake facing | 2 | $8.50 each | $54.50 each |
| Twin beds, Lavatory, lake facing | 2 | 7.00 each | 45.00 each |
| Double bed, private bath, lake facing | 2 | 8.00 each | 51.50 each |
| Double bed, Lavatory, lake facing | 2 | 6.50 each | 43.50 each |
| Double bed, Lavatory. Not lake facing | 2 | 6.00 each | 38.50 each |
| Single rooms, Lavatory. Not lake facing | 1 | 8.50 each | 56.50 each |

#### PRIVATE GUEST SLEEPING COTTAGES

| Description of Room | Number of Persons | American Plan | | European Plan—Meals Ala Carte | |
|---|---|---|---|---|---|
| | | Daily | Weekly | Daily | Weekly |
| 2 bedrooms, private bath | 4 | $6.00 each | $38.50 each | $8.00 for 4 | $52.50 for 4 |
| 2 bedrooms, private bath | 3 | 7.00 each | 45.50 each | 8.00 for 3 | 52.50 for 3 |
| 2 bedrooms, private bath | 2 | 8.00 each | 52.50 each | 8.00 for 2 | 52.50 for 2 |
| 1 bedroom, private bath, double bed | 2 | 7.50 each | 47.50 each | 7.00 for 2 | 45.00 for 2 |
| 1 bedroom, private bath, twin beds | 2 | 8.00 each | 52.50 each | 8.00 for 2 | 52.50 for 2 |
| 1 bedroom, private bath, twin beds, fireplace | 2 | 9.00 each | 59.50 each | 9.00 for 2 | 59.50 for 2 |
| 1 bedroom, private bath, 2 double beds, fireplace | 4 | 6.50 each | 39.50 each | 9.00 for 4 | 59.50 for 4 |

#### HOUSEKEEPING CABINS

| Description of Room | Number of Persons | | |
|---|---|---|---|
| 2 bedrooms, private bath, electric refrigerator, oil heat, gas for cooking | 4 or 5 | $9.00 per day | $55.00 per week |
| 2 bedroom, private bath, oil heat, gas for cooking | 3 or 4 | $7.50 per day | $45.00 per week |
| 1 bedroom, private toilet, gas for cooking, oil heat, electric refrigerator | 2 | $5.00 per day | $30.00 per week |

We Furnish All Linens, Dishes, Bedding, and Equipment

15% deduction from the above rates if your vacation is before June 25th or after September 25th. A $10.00 deposit is required on all reservations.

**A 1949 rate sheet for the lodge.**

[1] Letter and telephone conversation with Marilyn Mattson Nyquist on June 7, 2002.

**Back and front covers of what was probably Neudahl's 2nd brochure. 1941.**
*Above photo is from a copy of the original brochure.*

*Rustic bridge over Cascade River.*

# CASCADE LODGE . .

## A WONDERFUL PLACE

The Main Lodge is a beautiful hotel with a wide stone terrace across the front overlooking Lake Superior. Here in the Lodge is the attractive dining room, where the meals served are already famous for their excellence. A comfortable lounge with a large fireplace is provided for your rest and relaxation. The Lodge is about twenty feet above the level of the lake, and in back of it the wooded, rocky bluff rises to a height of one hundred feet above the lake level.

The log cabins, the finest that can be built, extend in two rows to one side and back up the bluff among the pines, and on either side of the mountain stream that tumbles down its rocky course to the lake. A rustic log bridge leads across the stream to the second row of cabins.

These cabins—all as secluded and delightfully located as a private summer home—are equipped with every convenience. Each has a screened-in porch, inside flush toilets, hot and cold running water, and electric lights.

Housekeeping cabins are equipped with Skelgas and are completely furnished, including ice and wood. Beds in lodge and cabins are equipped with innerspring mattresses.

SPORTS—Ping Pong and shuffle-board in recreation room. Tennis courts. Deep sea fishing on our cruiser. Beverages and dancing at Cascade Inn.

*Typical bedroom—Cascade Lodge.*

*Cascade River—short walk from the lodge.*

*Rustic modern cabin*

**Inside left panels of 1941 brochure. Note cabin 11 before new fireplace.**

## TO PLAY AND REST

FISHING—Lake and brook trout in all nearby lakes and streams. Good sport whipping the fly on Cascade River and other streams. Deep sea fishing on Lake Superior from cabin cruisers is available to those who like to catch the big ones. All deep sea fishing equipment is furnished and no license is required for non-residents.

HIKING—Numerous trails through Cascade Park and old logging roads through a wilderness country of beautiful scenery. Glorious days in woods and along streams.

KODAKING—Wonderful views and opportunities for pictures of game and wild life.

MOTORING—On broad, smooth, macadamized highways over the longest stretch of blue water highway in the world and on motor trails through virgin forests.

HUNTING—Bear, deer and an abundance of small game.

RESTING—A haven for hay fever sufferers. Cool nights and glorious days—with always a cool breeze from the lake—in the fragrant, piney air of the north woods.

BOATING—Motor boating on Superior or one of many nearby lakes—wonderful canoe trips on northern lakes.

RATES—American Plan—With or without bath as desired.

| | |
|---|---|
| Per day | $5.00 and up |
| Per week | $30.00 and up |

One-half rates for children under 6.

Housekeeping Cabins          $20.00 to $35.00 per week

Hotel rooms—single, $3.00 per night and up. Double, $3.50 per night and up. Meals served a la carte if preferred.

### CASCADE LODGE

H. Neudahl, Prop.     Telephone 15-R-1     Grand Marais, Minnesota

*Midway between Duluth and Port Arthur*

*Deep sea trolling—Lake Superior.*

*Dining room.*

*Above — Over twenty pound lake trout caught deep sea trolling.*

*Left—Very good deer hunting in this area.*

*Lounge.*

Inside right panels of 1941 brochure. Note: Rates were $5.00 and up for American Plan and Hotel rooms were $3.00 per night and up for a single room and $3.50 for two. House-keeping cabins were $20.00 to $35.00 per week.

Bus stops at our door.

Lake front, highway and corner of Cascade Lodge.

# CASCADE LODGE IN CASCADE STATE PARK

## ON NORTH SHORE OF LAKE SUPERIOR

*"A Friendly Spot in the Arrowhead"*

Here on America's most scenic highway, in the land of big game, big fish, and amidst the scenic grandeur of Cascade State Park, is located CASCADE LODGE, a new, modern, comfortable hotel with steam heated rooms, with or without private bath, and log cabin sleeping accommodations. Also housekeeping cabins for those who prefer. Whether you want to be alone or mingle with other congenial vacationists—here is the ideal spot —in the friendly atmosphere and beautiful surroundings of this wilderness resort of luxury and good comradeship.

Exactly halfway between Duluth and Port Arthur, on the famous North Shore Drive, this resort in the center of the north country—"The Playground of the World," is situated on the side of a bluff overlooking Lake Superior. The highway passes immediately in front

of the resort and within fifty feet of the rocky shore line.

This is one of the finest settings for a resort that can be imagined—a beautiful place of primeval wilderness on the shores of Lake Superior and beside the beautiful Cascade River, which winds its way thunderously through Cascade Park. The entire resort is backed up by a dense forest of pine, fir and birch. The changes that have been made in this rugged setting are simple and few, and only those essential to the complete comfort and convenience of visitors to Cascade Lodge and Cascade Park. The rugged beauty of this famous North Country has remained unspoiled. It is an ideal combination of natural beauty and comparative detachment from the outer world, and the necessary conveniences to wholehearted enjoyment of its beauties and of its opportunities for play and rest.

**First inside panels of a brochure. Note the picture of the bus stopping at the lodge.**
*Circa 1946 or 1947.*

## Brochures of the Forties

During the forties, at least three editions of the same basic black and white brochure were printed. Only slight changes were made at each printing. In what appears to be the 1947 edition, the photo of cabin 11 is changed to show the remodeled cabin with a new stone fireplace. A late forties edition shows an aerial view of the resort which includes the coffee shop/gas station building. Throughout the various editions of the 1940's brochures kodaking, motoring, hunting, hiking, fishing and resting continued to be activities that were highlighted with words or pictures.

As the decade of the forties came to an end Cascade Lodge was well established. The country had made the transition to a peace-time economy and tourism was on the rise. Through a great deal of hard work the Neudahls had developed the lodge into a significant business on the North Shore and they were well positioned to enter the fifties.

**Aerial photo of the lodge. There seems to be some type of building or shed between cabins 10 and 11. The large Standard gas sign evident in later pictures of the restaurant is not included in this picture. Note the sign in the lower left of the photo - shown close up in the next picture.** *Circa late 1940's or early 1950's.*

Old sign found in a shed in 1980's. The sign was originally located by the west driveway on the north side of the road. This sign most likely was put up when the first section of the new lodge was opening in 1939.

Sign by the lake which read as follows: "Dining Room / Cascade / Food at its Best." The sign was up from about 1947 to 1969.

[i] *"Cascade Lodge Has Grand Opening." Cook County News-Herald, May 11, 1939, p.1.*

[ii] *Interview with Irving Hansen by Gene Glader on March 11, 2003.*

[iii] *E. F. Lindquist, "Chamber of Commerce," Cook County News-Herald, June 11, 1942, p. 1.*

[iv] *"Local," Cook County News-Herald, February 19, 1942, p. 8. and "They say That..," Cook County News-Herald, March 26, 1942, p. 1.*

[v] *"Tourism Heads Discuss Gas Rationing Problem," Cook County News-Herald, June 4, 1942, p. 1.*

[vi] *"Gas Rationing Dates Now Set," Cook County News-Herald, November 5, 1942, p. 1.*

[vii] *"Traffic Deaths Down 54% Since 40-Mile Speed Law," Cook County News-Herald, August 13, 1942, p.1.*

[viii] *E. F. Lindquist, Secretary, "Chamber of Commerce, Cook County News-Herald, June 11, 1942, p. 1.*

[ix] *E. F. Lindquist, Secretary, Chamber of Commerce, Cook County News-Herald, September 3, 1942, P. 1.*

[x] *E. F. Lindquist, Secretary, "Chamber of Commerce, Cook County News-Herald, June 11, 1942, p. 1.*

[xi] *"Bakery to Close---No Sugar," Cook County News-Herald, August 29, 1946, p. 1.*

[xii] *Telephone interview by Gene Glader with former employee who requested to not be identified, June 28, 2003.*

[xiii] *"Junior-Senior Banquet Held at Cascade," Cook County News-Herald, June 3, 1943, p. 1.*

[xiv] *"Mrs. Stassen at Cascade," Cook County News-Herald, August 17, 1944, p.1.*

[xv] *"Grand Opening Dance Advertisement," Cook County News-Herald, June 12, 1947, p. 10.*

[xvi] *"July Fourth Dancing Advertisement," Cook County News-Herald, July 3, 1947, p. 10.*

[xvii] *"Lloyd Johnson, Carl Ertsgard, Jr. Top Skiers," Cook County News-Herald, March 6, 1947, p.1.*

[xviii] *"So You Want to be a Skier," Cook County News-Herald, December 30, 1948., p. 11.*

[xix] *"Nelsons Open Ski Area; Ask Help in Housing Visiting Skiers," Cook County News-Herald, December 23, 1948, p. 1.*

[xx] *"World's Champion to Appear at New Skate Rink," Cook County News-Herald, December 1, 1949, p. 1.*

# The Fifties and Sixties

## Chapter VII

### A New Decade Begins

The fifties were generally considered a stable and prosperous time in our country. Granted the Korean Conflict (War) during the early fifties and the Cold War were national concerns; nevertheless, life for most citizens was good. Highways continued to be improved, manufacturers continued to turn out bigger and better cars and gas was cheap. All of this contributed to a growing tourism industry.

Regarding the Neudahl family, LaVerne had gone off to college at Hamline University in the fall of 1949 and Elvira married Wilford Miller in 1950 in Memphis, Tennessee, where Wilford was working at the time. They had met during her trips to Hot Springs, Arkansas when Wilford was working there. During the summer of 1951 LaVerne was selected as the "Miss North Shore" queen as part of the Grand Marais Fishermen's Picnic festivities.[i]

**College graduation photo of LaVerne Neudahl in 1954.** *Photo courtesy Valaine Robinet.*

After Elvira and Wilford Miller were married they returned to work at the lodge during the summer of 1950 and perhaps again during the summer of 1951. They lived in St. Paul, for a short time after their marriage and then, in 1955 moved permanently to Florida. Elvira continued to come back each summer to help her parents run the resort until it was sold in 1969. She worked mainly in the office and the dining room. Even though she had little or no muscular control of her lower limbs, she had developed an amazing ability to get around with the use of her crutches and a wheel chair. Her husband, Wilford, recalled that for many years she even drove the car between Cascade and Florida when she returned to help at the lodge.[ii]

## The West Wing is Added to the Main Lodge

By 1952 the lodge had been serving guests for twenty-five years and had become well established as a popular resort on the North Shore. At about this time the Neudahls began to think that it was time to add the west wing to the lodge. It was completed during the summer of 1957.[1] The entire main lodge was winterized, except for the absence of insulation in the walls and above the second floor ceiling. The new addition consisted of four new rental rooms on the second floor, a two-bedroom apartment with a kitchen and living room for the owners on the first floor, and a basement shop and garage area. The completion of the apartment in the new west wing gave the Neudahls a very nice place to live as a family. When the new space for the Neudahl family was completed, the first floor room next to the main fireplace was converted to a guest room.

---

[1] This date is mentioned in the real estate sales listing of the property during the late 1960's.

**Postcard photo of the lodge with completed west wing.** *Circa 1958.*

## The Dining Room is Relocated to the Coffee Shop Building

Also during this period, most likely in 1956 or 1957, additional kitchen space was added to the back of the coffee shop. The new kitchen space made it possible to move the dining room out of the main lodge and change the coffee shop to the Cascade Lodge Dining Room. When the dining room was in the main lodge, service was available for limited periods of time for breakfast, lunch and dinner. With the relocation of the dining room to the coffee shop, meals and snacks were served all day and into the evening. The dining room was always under the direct supervision of Mrs. Neudahl. In the late fifties or early sixties the lodge quit selling gasoline, and the gas pumps and the gas signs were removed.

The Coffee Shop /Restaurant was not winterized. The walls and ceiling were devoid of any insulation and the water pipes to the building were above ground. Consequently, the restaurant was never open during the winter while the Neudahls operated the lodge. Whether it was open past Labor Day in the fall during the fifties and sixties is not certain.

**Cascade Dining Room. Note sign on building, west wing of lodge and gas pumps, Standard Oil sign and new picture windows on lake side of dining room.** *Circa 1957. Photo courtesy of Valaine Robinet.*

**Interior of the new Cascade Dining Room.** *Photo courtesy of Valaine Robinet.*

**Exterior of restaurant as it appeared in the late 1950's or 1960's. Photo from a postcard.**

With the transfer of the dining room to the coffee shop building the former dining space in the main lodge was converted into a large living room area and the kitchen area into two rental apartments. In order to create enough space for the two apartments a small one floor addition was added to the northeast corner of the lodge. Each apartment had a small kitchen area, bedroom and bathroom. Originally the corner apartment was called apartment 1 and the other one was called apartment 2. Now the units are numbered 101 and 103. Room 103 was converted to a staff room in 2000.

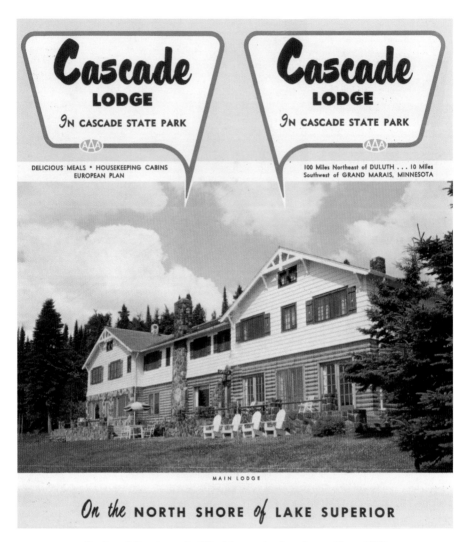

**Back and front panel of first four-color brochure.** *Circa 1958.*

CASCADE LODGE
In Cascade State Park

Here on America's most scenic highway, in the land of big game, big fish, and amidst the scenic grandeur of Cascade State Park, is located CASCADE LODGE.

At Cascade Lodge you may rest or take part in active sports, just as you wish. If you like action, the following activities are here:

FISHING—Good sport whipping the fly on Cascade River and other nearby streams. Deep Sea Fishing on Lake Superior is available to those who like to catch the big ones. All deep-sea equipment and a licensed captain is furnished. Also inland lake fishing for Walleyed Pike, Great Northern Pike, Land-locked Salmon, and other Pan Fish on any of the numerous lakes within a radius of 25 miles.

HIKING—Numerous trails through Cascade State Park and along old logging roads through a wilderness country of breath-taking loveliness. Delicious picnic lunches are available to those who desire them.

KODAKING—Wonderful views and opportunities for pictures of scenery and wild life.

MOTORING—On broad, smooth, macadamized highways over the longest stretch of blue-water highway in the world and on motor trails through virgin forests.

HUNTING—Deer, bear, and an abundance of small game in season.

RESTING—A haven for hay-fever sufferers. Cool nights and glorious days—with a cool breeze from the lake always—in the fragrant piney air of the North Woods.

For your further amusement and enjoyment we have Ping-pong, shuffleboard, and croquet. Tennis courts are nearby.

Plan to spend your vacation at:

**CASCADE LODGE**
Mr. and Mrs. H. Neudahl, Proprietors
Telephone 28-R-2
P. O. GRAND MARAIS, MINNESOTA

**Inside left panels of brochure. Note: the aerial photo is older and shows the lodge without the west addition.** *Circa 1958.*

CASCADE LODGE
*Accommodations*

Cascade Lodge is a modern new lodge—it is truly the finest on the North Shore; it is not a large place by metropolitan standards, but its owners are friendly people and those who stay at Cascade are friendly folk.

Guests dress and live their vacation in a relaxed and easy manner. You are invited to spend your vacation in this atmosphere.

The Main Lodge is a beautiful hotel with a wide stone terrace across the front overlooking Lake Superior. Guests enjoy evenings in the spacious game room, where Television, cards, checkers, and scrabble are provided. There is also a basement rumpus room where ping-pong, shuffleboard, and bumper pool are furnished. A comfortable lounge with a large fireplace is provided for your rest and relaxation. The Lodge is about fifty feet above the level of the lake, and in back of it the wooded, rocky bluff rises to a height of several hundred feet.

The log cabins, the finest that can be built, extend in two rows to one side and back up the bluff among the pines, and on either side of the mountain stream that tumbles down its rocky course to the lake. A rustic log bridge leads across the stream to the second row of cabins.

These cabins—all as secluded and delightfully located as a private summer home—are equipped with every convenience. Each has a screened-in porch, inside flush toilet, shower, hot and cold running water, and electric lights. Some have fireplaces.

This is one of the finest settings for a resort that can be imagined—a beautiful place of primeval wilderness on the shores of Lake Superior and beside the beautiful Cascade River, which winds its way thunderously through Cascade Park. The entire resort is backed up by a dense forest of pine, fir and birch. The changes that have been made in this rugged setting are simple and few and only those essential to the complete comfort and convenience of visitors to Cascade Lodge and Cascade Park. The rugged beauty of this famous North Country has remained unspoiled. It is an ideal combination of natural beauty and comparative detachment from the outer world and of the necessary conveniences to wholehearted enjoyment of its beauties and its opportunities for play and rest.

**Inside right panels in brochure.** *Circa 1958.*

## *Cascade Lodge* ON THE
## NORTH SHORE *of*
## LAKE SUPERIOR

The North Shore Drive of Lake Superior extends from Duluth, Minnesota, to Port Arthur, Ontario, a distance of 206 miles. Half way on this drive (99.7 miles from Duluth) is located CASCADE LODGE, a new, modern, comfortable hotel with steam-heated rooms (with or without bath) and private guest sleeping cabins (all with private bath).

No drive in the country is more famous for its beauty than the North Shore Drive. Following closely the shoreline of Lake Superior, U. S. Highway No. 61 wends its way through hilly, virgin areas of breath-taking loveliness.

Lofty evergreens, deep green valleys, rushing streams and waterfalls, the vast cool waters of the great lake where boats sail day and night . . . all this and more in a vacation wonderland that never grows monotonous.

COOL NIGHTS . . . GORGEOUS DAYS
Nowhere on the continent are nights so cool and restful as on the North Shore. Here you sleep under blankets every night. Bring your sweaters and don't forget hiking boots and slacks.

If you don't care to drive, Greyhound buses make two trips daily from Duluth, with stops at Cascade Lodge.

CASCADE DINING ROOM AND COFFEE SHOP operated in connection with Cascade lodge is open to the public—serving delicious meals or snacks from 7 A.M. to 9 P.M.—Is under the direct supervision of Mrs. Neudahl who is famous on the North Shore for Good Food at Moderate Prices.

**Two of the inside panels in the first four-color brochure. Note that the Greyhound bus made two trips daily with stops at Cascade Lodge.** *Circa 1958.*

103

**Dine Out Tonight or**
**Any Night**

at

# Cascade Lodge
# Restaurant

serving your favorite steaks, chicken,
fish and sea foods

also

**Specials Every Night**

from 5 p.m. to 10 p.m.

Thursday — Breaded Veal Cutlet Parmesan — $1.85

Friday — Fillet of Lake Superior Blue Fin — $1.75

Saturday — Roast Prime Ribs of Beef — $2.90
or
Baked Meat Loaf — $1.60

Sunday (from 12:00 noon) Roast Young Tom Turkey — $1.90

Monday — Browned Rolled Round Steak Saute' — $1.85

Tuesday — Country Fried Spring Chicken — $1.75

Wednesday — Roast Sirloin of Beef — $1.95

Advertisement in <u>Cook County News-Herald</u> on July 9, 1959.

**Three-unit motel built between 1961 and 1965.** *Photo courtesy of Valaine Robinet.*

## A Motel is Added to the Lodging Options

The last building project undertaken by the Neudahls was the addition of a three-unit motel. It was a non-winterized building built behind the site occupied by Cabin 5. Cabin 5 was removed either before or after the construction of the motel and the land on which it was located became the parking area for the motel. With the removal of Cabin 5 the motel rooms became numbers 5A, 5B & 5C. The construction date of the motel was most likely 1961, but some evidence indicates a date as late as 1965.

**Side view of motel. Note that the building is constructed without a full, winterized foundation.**

**Herbert and Minnie Neudahl** *Circa 1960. Photo Courtesy of Valaine Robinet.*

## Winter Vacations for the Neudahls

During the late forties until sometime in the sixties the Neudahls traveled to Florida or other southern states for a month or more most winters. Confirmation of their winter vacations comes from both the local newspaper and former employees. Martin Vensland, who worked as a bartender and handyman for the Neudahls from 1950 to 1953, recalled that the Neudahls closed the lodge between the end of the deer hunting season and April 1, and spent their winters in Florida during those years.[iii] An example of the local newspaper reports on these trips appeared in the March 15, 1959 edition of the paper. On this date the newspaper reported that Mr. and Mrs. Neudahl had returned from a three month stay in Vero Beach, Florida where they visited Elvira. LaVerne was with them, but she stayed longer in Florida.[iv] From such visits to Florida, LaVerne met her future husband, Paul Bishop. They were married at Fort Pierce Beach on December 26, 1960.[v] Since the restaurant and cabins were never open in the winter such a vacation schedule was possible.

## Major Highway Improvements

Significant highway development between the Twin Cities and Two Harbors enhanced the tourism business for Cascade Lodge and other resorts on the North Shore during the sixties. The construction of Interstate Highway 35 between the Twin Cites and Duluth was a major improvement in transportation. This road was built in sections over approximately a ten-year period. The first section opened in 1962 and the last section entering Duluth, was finished in about 1968. The connection to Mesabi Avenue in Duluth was finished in about 1972.

The second major highway improvement during the 1960's was the construction of the expressway between Duluth and Two Harbors, which began in 1962. The road was opened in sections and was finished in 1967. The expressway gave motorists the option of a faster route between the two cities or a more leisurely scenic route on old highway 61 along the shore. Going through Duluth remained a "bottle neck," until 1992 when the freeway by the lake was completed.

In addition to the great importance of the two highway sections mentioned above, it is important to acknowledge the significance of the entire freeway system that was being built across the nation during the late 1950's and 1960's. Not only did the new freeways enhance the economy in general, they helped stimulate the emerging tourism sector of the U.S. economy. More specifically, the freeways leading to Minnesota made it much easier for tourists to visit the North Shore from a wider geographic area.

## Winter Business at the Lodge

Lodge rooms were rented to skiers on a limited basis during the winters of the fifties and sixties. It is very doubtful that the lodge was open for guests when the Neudahls went south for their annual vacation. Consequently, their involvement in the beginning of winter tourism on the shore was fairly limited. This view is supported by a statement by a realtor, in his descriptive material about the lodge in the spring of 1969. Len Hedman had the lodge listed for sale during 1968 and early 1969, and wrote as follows about the winter business at the lodge:

"Although for the past few years the resort has been operated only in the summer, there is a tremendous potential for a year round business catering to skiers in the winter. Rental income from skiers' rooms only, last winter, exceeded $5,000 and this could be tripled by serving meals."[vi]

**Side view showing the addition to the back of the restaurant. Note addition of restaurant sign on top of the building.** *Photo by Len Hedman March 1969.*

## Difficult Times for the Family

In the spring of 1963 Mr. and Mrs. Neudahl's adult son, Herbert August, was killed in an automobile accident in Minneapolis. This was their third child to die and the second of their two sons. Herbert August Neudahl had five children and lived in the Twin Cities at the time of his death. Throughout the years he had also worked at the lodge. During the late sixties the Neudahl's daughter, LaVerne, came home from Florida with her two small children to help at the lodge in the summers. LaVerne's daughter Valaine was born in 1962 and she remembers that she and her brother and mother came to the lodge every summer when she was a little girl. She specifically recalls beginning kindergarten and first grade in the Grand Marais Elementary School and moving back to Florida in late September or early October.[vii] This had to be the school years of 1967 - 68 or 1968 - 69. During these years the Neudahls would certainly have benefited from some extra family help.

On September 18, 1968 Herbert F. Neudahl passed away at the age of 76. His health had been failing for a couple of years. Mr. Neudahl apparently had been quite involved in the construction of the restaurant building and the west wing of the lodge, in addition to many other roles he must have assumed as co-owner with his wife. It is not known whether the Neudahls had tried to sell the lodge prior to Herbert's death. It is known that by the spring of 1969 Mrs. Neudahl had listed the resort with a realtor for $130,000.00. The realtor reported gross income ranging from $44,600 in 1955 to figures around $30,000 from 1964 to 1968. One can only speculate why the figure is so much higher in 1955. Perhaps the lodge was open later in the fall and earlier in the spring during the fifties. It does appear that the lodge was closed for longer periods of time as the Neudahls got older and perhaps took longer vacations. The realtor also reported that the Neudahls had a staff of ten people during the summer.

## The Lodge is Sold

On October 22, 1969 Mrs. Neudahl sold the lodge to Mr. and Mrs. Michael Rusten of Plymouth, Minnesota. This concluded 34 ½ years of ownership by the Neudahls, plus an additional year of leasing and managing the lodge in 1934. At the time of the sale Mrs. Neudahl was 77 years of age. There is little doubt that Minnie Neudahl was the driving force behind the lodge. She was the boss. She and her husband were hard workers who developed the lodge into one of the well known, quality resorts in Northeastern Minnesota. The lodge has probably been approved by the American Automobile Association (AAA) longer than any resort in the area. The sale of the lodge in 1969 marked the end of an era in which the lodge was open only on a seasonal basis.

# CASCADE LODGE... *A friendly spot in the Arrowhead*

MIDWAY BETWEEN DULUTH AND PORT ARTHUR ON HIGHWAY U. S. 61

**Modern Cabins · Excellent Meals**

**GRAND MARAIS · MINNESOTA**

\*\*\*\*\*\*\*ROOM RATES\*\*\*\*\*\*\*\*\*\*\*\*\*\*\*\*\*\*\*\*\*\*

Main Lodge\*\*\*\*\*\*\*\*

Room Number\*\*\*\*
```
***101***1st Floor 2 Single Beds****  10.00 plus 30¢ Sales Tax--- $10.30
*** 201**2nd Floor 1 D 1 S   "  ****   10.50 plus 32¢  "     "  --- 10.82 Corner Room
*** 202**2nd Floor 2 Double Beds ***   14.00 plus 42¢  "     "  --- 14.42 Corner Room
*** 204***      "  3 Single Beds ***   12.00 plus 36¢  "     "----  12.36
*** 205 **      "  1 Double Bed ****    8.00 plus 24¢  "     "  ---  8.24
*** 206 **      "  1 Double Bed ****    6.00 plus 18¢  "     "  ---  6.18 No bath or Toilet
*** 207 **      "  1 Double Bed ****    6.00 plus 18¢  "     "  ---  6.18 No bath or Toilet
*** 208 **      "  2 Single Beds ***   10.00 plus 30¢  "     "  --- 10.30
*** 209 **      "  1 Double bed ****    8.00 plus 24¢  "     "  ---  8.24
*** 210 **      "  1 Double Bed ****    9.00 plus 27¢  "     "  ---  9.27
*** 211 **      "  2 Single Beds ***   10.00 plus 30¢  "     "  --- 10.30
*** 212 **      "  2 Double Beds ***   12.00 plus 36¢  "     "  --- 12.36 for two persons
                                       14.00 plus 42¢  "     "---- 14.42 for Three or Four
*** 214 **  "      2 Double Beds ***   14.00 plus 42¢  "     "  --- 14.42 for two persons
                                       16.00 plus 48¢  "     "  --- 14.48 for three or four
*** 215*** "        1 D 1 S            10.50 plus 32¢  "    "  --- 10.82 for two persons
                                       12.00 plus 36¢  "    "  --- 12.36for three persons

Apt. 1 Housekeeping Main Floor  2 S   12.00 plus 36¢  "    "  --- 12.36
       For Sleeping Only              10.00 plus 30¢  "    "  --- 10.30
Apt. 2 Housekeeping Main Floor 1 D    12.00 plus 36¢  "    "  --- 12.36
       For Sleeping Only              10.00 plus 30¢  "    "  --- 10.30
```

All even number rooms face lake, Odd number rooms faces the hill view

CABIN RATES

Cabin Number\*\*\*\*\*\*
```
1             2 double beds        10.50 plus  32¢ sales tax -- 10.82
2             4  "      "          14.00 plus  48¢  "    "   -- 14.42
3             4  "      "          14.00 plus  48¢  "    "   -- 14.48
4             1  "      "           6.00 plus  18¢  "    "   --  6.18
5 A, B, C     2 singles each unit  10.00 plus  30¢  "    "   -- 10.30 each unit
6       1 D  2 S Housekeeping      14.00 plus  42¢  "    "   -- 14.42
7       1 D  1 S Housekeeping      11.00 plus  33¢  "    "   -- 11.33
8       1 D  1 S                   10.50 plus  32¢  "    "   -- 10.82
8B      1 Double Bed                8.00 plus  24¢  "    "   --  8.24
9       1 Double 1 Fold Up         10.00 plus  30¢  "    "   -- 10.30 for two persons
                                   12.00 plus  36¢  "    "   -- 12.36 for four persons
10      1 Double 1 Single, 1 folding  14.00 plus 42¢  "  "   -- 14.42
```

At checkin time guest will pay in advance for rooms or cabinss assigned to,
registration must be marked paid and initialed.

The above was apparently an in-house, front desk rate sheet. It was most likely for the summer of 1969. Note: Cabin 8 is today's Cabin 9, Cabin 8B is today's Cabin 8 and Cabin 9 is today's Cabin 11.

[i] *"LAVERNE NEUDAHL NEW 'MISS NORTH SHORE',"* <u>*Cook County News-Herald,*</u> *August 8, 1951, p. 1.*

[ii] *Telephone Interview with Wilford Miller by Gene Glader on June 6, 2002.*

[iii] *Interview with Martin Vensland by Milford J. Humphrey, March 31, 1983.*

[iv] *"Shore Lines,"* <u>*Cook County News-Herald,*</u> *March 15, 1959, p. 8*

[v] *"LaVerne Neudahl Bride of Paul W. Bishop,"* <u>*Cook County News-Herald,*</u> *January 19, 1961, p. 2.*

[vi] *"North Shore Resort-Hotel," Description of property by Hedman's Resort Exchange, Grand Rapids, Minnesota, 1968.*

[vii] *Telephone Interview with Valaine Robinet by Gene Glader on June 6, 2002.*

# The Fifties and Sixties

## *The Rusten and Odmark Years*

# Chapter VIII

### The Rustens Discover Cascade Lodge

During the late 1960's Michael Rusten was working as an assistant pastor at Calvary Memorial Church in the Navare area of Orono, Minnesota. The position included directing a one or two week camp for the church kids of upper elementary school age through junior high age. Coinciding with Mike's interest in Christian camp work, he had begun to do some thinking about the possibility of buying a resort. This interest was strong enough to have caused him to begin looking for newspaper advertisements of resorts for sale during the spring of 1969.

As the camp sessions were nearing an end during the summer of 1969, Mike felt that it was time for him to move on and do something else. He had no specific future plans; nevertheless, he asked for a leave of absence from his position at the church. When the camp sessions were over, Mike and his wife, Sharon, whom he had met at the church, drove up to Grand Marais for a brief vacation. Mike and Sharon had become familiar with Grand Marais in earlier years when they had visited Mike's aunt, who had previously been the school librarian in Grand Marais.

As they passed Cascade Lodge on the way to Grand Marais, Mike said to Sharon, " Now if that place was for sale, that would be the one to buy." They stayed at the Shoreline Motel in Grand Marais, and while they were there, they checked out two resorts on the Gunflint Trail that were for sale, but neither matched what they were looking for. On Friday they decided to go to Lutsen Resort for dinner. As they drove past Cascade Lodge, all of a sudden they noticed a "For Sale" sign on the lawn and quickly turned around and drove up to the lodge to make an appointment to meet the owners. They introduced themselves to Mrs. Neudahl and made an appointment to tour the lodge the next day. As they toured the property they both became impressed with the possibilities at the lodge. After the meeting with Mrs. Neudahl, Mike and Sharon began their trip home to Plymouth, Minnesota, since this was the last day of their vacation. On the way they discussed the possibility of buying Cascade Lodge, but knew that they would need some specific help in order to make it work. They agreed that they would need to find a skilled maintenance person and a restaurant manager before they could go ahead with any efforts to purchase the lodge. The only person they could think of who might be a candidate for running the restaurant was Bill Thomas, who was an elder at their church. They thought of him because he often cooked at steak fries for the men of the church and his steaks were unusually good.

The next morning after the church service they saw Bill Thomas and mentioned to him that they had just returned from the North Shore. Bill said, "We just came back from there also. In fact, we just purchased some land up there." Mike asked him if perhaps he had ever worked as a chef. Bill's answer was that cooking was his first love and only through a series of circumstances had he become a butcher. So Mike and Sharon began to wonder if Bill could be a candidate for managing the restaurant at Cascade. Then they told Sharon's parents, Carl and Mae Odmark about the lodge. Mike and Sharon valued Carl's knowledge about buildings and remodeling so they asked Carl to come up and look the lodge over with them. Mike and Sharon soon visited the lodge again and while there, Carl flew to Duluth, where they picked him up and took him to the resort. After looking at the lodge, Carl concurred that the place had great possibilities.

Mike had earlier graduated from Princeton University and was currently busy working on his dissertation for a Ph.D. in religious education at New York University. Consequently, the possibility of hiring someone else to manage the day-to-day operation of the lodge also began to appeal to Mike and Sharon. In addition they still needed a person to oversee physical maintenance and development in order to go forward with any effort to purchase the property. Eventually their thoughts again turned to Sharon's dad, Carl. They knew Carl had the skills necessary to manage the lodge, but they also thought that Carl would probably not be interested in moving because he was so active in the local community. He was a partner, with another man, in a heating and air conditioning business, chairman of Calvary Memorial Church, a Scoutmaster, board member of an area vocational-technical school program and very active in civic affairs in Mound. Nevertheless, Mike and Sharon decided to ask Carl if he would be willing to manage the lodge. To their surprise Carl said, "To tell you the truth, my secret desire has always been to run a resort." His wife, Mae wasn't quite as excited about the idea, but she agreed to be a part of the team if Carl wanted to do it. So Carl and Mae Odmark agreed to become the managers of the lodge if Mike and Sharon purchased it.

The next step was to talk to Bill and Lois Thomas to see if Bill would be interested in managing the restaurant if Mike and Sharon bought the resort. Bill indicated again that he had often thought about being a cook and managing a restaurant. He also said he would be willing to accept the job, if the Rustens' dream materialized. Since Bill and Lois already loved the North Shore, it was not hard to convince Lois to participate.

**Sharon and Michael Rusten with their daughter Marta. 1970.** *Photo courtesy of the Rustens.*

With the key personnel in place Mike and Sharon purchased the lodge on October 22, 1969. Mike and Sharon immediately moved up to the lodge and settled into the apartment which the Neudahls had occupied. Carl Odmark soon sold his share of the heating and air conditioning business to his partner and began making plans to join them. In December he and Mae moved to the lodge, temporarily sharing the first floor apartment with Mike and Sharon. Mae, who was co-manager of the lodge with Carl, initially became the primary front desk receptionist and what probably could be called the head housekeeper, although she never had that title. During the next few months the Rustens and Odmarks worked closely together mapping out the future plans for the lodge. Thus the transition of ownership and management from the Neudahls to the Rustens and Odmarks began.

**115**

**Mae and Carl Odmark. Circa 1975.** *Photo courtesy of Mike & Sharon Rusten.*

## Remodeling the Restaurant

The new owners first major decision was to transform Cascade into a year around facility. Step one in the process was the remodeling and winterizing of the restaurant. Since the restaurant had always been closed during the winter, this was a natural place to start that first December. Carl Odmark was a very skilled and experienced craftsman, which was a great asset during this period. The remodeling of the restaurant involved adding insulation in the attic space, building new wooden beams for the interior of the dining room, installing a furnace, replacing some equipment in the kitchen, updating the electrical service and replacing the light fixtures. Earlier, Mike's father, Dr. Elmer Rusten had collected some vintage wagon wheels, which he gave to the lodge for Carl to use to make chandeliers for the restaurant and lodge. Dr. and Mrs. Rusten then loaned the lodge a wonderful collection of trophy fish and animal mounts for display. Dr. Rusten had accumulated the collection from various hunting and fishing trips to Alaska and the Northwest Territory of Canada starting in the 1940's. Mrs. Elmer Rusten and Mike had gone along on some of these trips. The remodeling and redecorating gave a new northwoods atmosphere to the restaurant.

**A postcard of the remodeled interior of the restaurant with the wagon wheel chandeliers and ceiling beams built by Carl Odmark.** *Circa 1971.*

## The First Winter for the New Owners

The transition to a year-round resort began modestly since only the main lodge was available for winter lodging. During that first winter of ownership, 1969-70, there was a high level of occupancy between Christmas and New Years and on weekends from the third weekend in January through February. Demand for rooms was so high that two dorm-type rooms with bunk beds were rented in the basement of the main lodge, and rooms in the motel, which had no running water in the winter, were rented out a few times. The motel rooms were not rented out again in the winter until the building was winterized.

The first Christmas/New Years period was a real challenge for the Rustens and Odmarks since everything at the lodge was new to them. During this first busy week with the lodge full of guests the sewage pipe from the main lodge to the holding tank froze, creating unworkable or overflowing toilets throughout the building. Adding to the problem was the fact that no one knew where the blocked and frozen pipe was located under the snow. Carl eventually localized the problem and called Irving Hansen at Isak Hansen and Sons, a local hardware store, and told him he had a real problem on his hands and needed his help. Irving, as he has done for many people over the years, changed his plans and brought an employee, Curt Pederson over with him and helped Carl remove the obstruction. In order to melt the frozen obstruction Curt Pederson climbed down into the large holding tank and pushed the equipment, either an auger or hot water hose, into the sewage pipe from the holding tank. All of a sudden, the obstruction broke lose and hundreds of gallons of sewage rushed from the two story lodge building directly toward Curt. Fortunately, Curt was able to quickly move to the ladder and climb out through the manhole. He probably remembered that experience the rest of his life.

The demand for rooms on the peak weekends during the winter of 1969-70 was primarily due to the number of people coming to ski at the Lutsen Ski Area. There simply wasn't enough lodging available in the area to accommodate the number of skiers desiring to ski on busy weekends. Yet from Sunday through Thursday there was virtually no business. In fact during the week, hours would pass without a single vehicle driving by the lodge.

**118**

## A New Marketing Plan and Image

Shortly after purchasing the lodge Mike contacted his friend, Steve Martin of the Martin-Williams Advertising agency, for help in developing a marketing plan for the lodge. They worked out a trade arrangement by which key employees of the agency, and their families, could stay at the lodge in exchange for work performed by the agency. This arrangement made it possible for the agency personnel to become more acquainted with the lodge and area and thus get a better feel for the image they wanted to project in their plans. The trade arrangement was so effective that it remained in use until 2004. The trade arrangement from 1981 to 2004 was with Homer Eclov, a former employee of the Martin-Williams firm. In 1970 the Martin-Williams agency was very small, but over the years grew to become a well-known advertising agency in Minneapolis. At the time when the initial marketing strategy was formulated, Don Hagg was the creative director and Ken Morrison was the artistic director. By spring Ken Morrison had created the new logo for the lodge, which has become a well recognized symbol on the North Shore. Prior to this no logo had been used at the lodge. Steve Martin strongly recommended to the Rustens and Odmarks that the new sign with the new logo be put up as soon as possible in the spring of 1970. With the new logo in place a whole new image of the resort began to emerge. The new image and design were incorporated in the lodge stationary, menu covers, brochures and signage of the lodge. In devising a redecorating scheme, the Rustens and Odmarks worked closely with designer Jack Bratrud, who formulated plans for remodeling both the restaurant and the lodge lobby and living rooms.

**The New Logo.**

**The new sign with the new logo on the front lawn.**

For the first summer a simple three-color brochure was developed with the new logo on the cover. In addition, a new little wallet sized folding rate card was designed.

**The back and front panel of the new rate card summer 1970.**

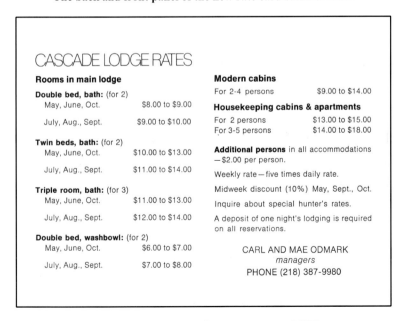

## CASCADE LODGE RATES

**Rooms in main lodge**

**Double bed, bath:** (for 2)

| | |
|---|---|
| May, June, Oct. | $8.00 to $9.00 |
| July, Aug., Sept. | $9.00 to $10.00 |

**Twin beds, bath:** (for 2)

| | |
|---|---|
| May, June, Oct. | $10.00 to $13.00 |
| July, Aug., Sept. | $11.00 to $14.00 |

**Triple room, bath:** (for 3)

| | |
|---|---|
| May, June, Oct. | $11.00 to $13.00 |
| July, Aug., Sept. | $12.00 to $14.00 |

**Double bed, washbowl:** (for 2)

| | |
|---|---|
| May, June, Oct. | $6.00 to $7.00 |
| July, Aug., Sept. | $7.00 to $8.00 |

**Modern cabins**

| | |
|---|---|
| For 2-4 persons | $9.00 to $14.00 |

**Housekeeping cabins & apartments**

| | |
|---|---|
| For 2 persons | $13.00 to $15.00 |
| For 3-5 persons | $14.00 to $18.00 |

**Additional persons** in all accommodations —$2.00 per person.

Weekly rate—five times daily rate.

Midweek discount (10%) May, Sept., Oct.

Inquire about special hunter's rates.

A deposit of one night's lodging is required on all reservations.

CARL AND MAE ODMARK
*managers*
PHONE (218) 387-9980

**Inside of new rate card for the summer of 1970.**

## Key New Staff Arrive

By the spring of 1970 Bill and Lois Thomas had sold their house in Mound and moved up to the area. Bill began working at the lodge on April

1st. His first task was to get the restaurant and menu ready for the summer. It was not until October of 1973 that Lois began working for the lodge as a bookkeeper and front desk receptionist. The restaurant re-opened for Memorial Day Weekend in 1970 and has remained open ever since, with the exception of short periods in November and April. In addition to the interior design changes in the restaurant, the new owners decided to discontinue selling alcoholic beverages at the restaurant and lodge.

**Bill Thomas in Cascade Restaurant.** *Circa early 1980's.*

In September of 1970 Janis Clark, along with her two youngest children, moved from Minneapolis and joined the lodge staff. Janis was already well acquainted with the Odmarks since one of her older daughters was married to Jim Odmark, the son of Carl and Mae. Cabin 6 was quickly winterized so Janis and her daughters could use it as their year-round home. Initially, Janis helped out in several areas such as housekeeping, waitressing and gift shop management. After a few months she started working with Bill Thomas in the restaurant and soon became his lead cook.

**Janis Clark Photo 1982.**

## Mike and Sharon Move Back to Minneapolis Area

In the fall of 1970, after living on site at the lodge for about a year, Mike and Sharon moved back to the Minneapolis area. They both continued to work on many lodge projects including marketing, finances, staffing and future plans for the resort. Mike also continued to work on his doctoral dissertation. They returned to the lodge most weekends, especially during the summers. In 1974 they started a greeting card company called Morning Star, which occupied much of their time.

## Frozen Water Pipes

Some time during the spring or fall of 1970 Carl had heavy equipment brought onto the lodge property to dig a trench for an underground water pipe from the lodge to the restaurant. Prior to winterization of the restaurant, the water pipes had been above ground. The project involved solving two problems. The first was digging a trench deep enough so that the water pipe would not freeze in the winter. Since bedrock is so close to the surface on most of the lodge property the trench ended up being only 2.5 to 5 feet deep in places. The solution to the lack of ground cover was to surround the pipe with plenty of insulation. The second problem involved crossing the creek with the pipe and not having the water freeze. The first effort involved putting the water pipe inside a larger pipe and laying it on the bottom of the creek with rocks and gravel on top. Unfortunately the pipe froze during the next Christmas season at a time when the restaurant had lots of customers. To temporarily solve the problem Carl connected a garden hose from the lodge and ran it across the creek to the restaurant. However, after a short period of time the garden hose also froze. Then Carl replaced the first garden hose with a second garden hose and with Mae's help thawed out the first garden hose in a laundry tub. The hoses kept freezing while the restaurant was open so Carl and Mae kept switching and thawing out the hoses to get through the weekend. For the remainder of the winter a temporary above-ground pipe and/or hose, which was wrapped with a heat tape or wire, was used to supply water to the restaurant. This solved the problem for the remainder of the winter. The following summer a new electrically heated wire was pushed into the water pipe where it crossed the creek. The heat wire has kept the water pipe from freezing ever since.

## The Project List

There were always plenty of projects to keep the Odmarks and Rustens busy during the first couple of transitional years. The number of projects was compounded by the desire to upgrade the facilities and convert the lodge into a year around business. Two of the new projects involved insulating the attic of the main lodge and installing new decorative ceiling beams in the lodge living rooms and wagon wheel chandeliers in the fireplace room and lobby. Carl also crafted and installed the copper mantel over the fireplace in the main lodge during this period.

**Copper fireplace mantel, chandelier and ceiling beams crafted by Carl Odmark in the lodge living room.**

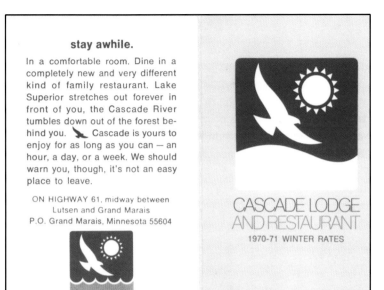

Outside panels of new 1970-71 winter rate card. A winter variation of the logo was designed for used in some winter materials.

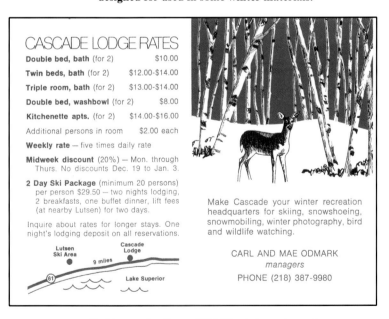

Inside panels of new 1970-71 winter rate card.

125

## Feeding the Deer

During the winter the deer living in the woods along the shore of Lake Superior migrate closer to the lake where the temperature tends to be a bit warmer and where the snow isn't quite as deep as it is around Deeryard Lake. In the spring the deer tend to move back further into the woods again. After observing this pattern of behavior during 1969-70 the Odmarks began putting out some alfalfa hay each day behind the lodge for the deer to eat during the winter. This proved to be a pleasant daily sight for guests and staff. The deer are still given about one-half bale of hay each day once snow has covered the ground. In the course of a typical day eight to thirty deer may show up for an easy breakfast or lunch.

**Harold Piepho feeding the deer some alfalfa hay in the morning behind the lodge.**

## The Douglas Shortley Memorial

During May of 1971, Carl took on a project that held very special meaning for him. He and some former scouts and leaders from Carl's scout troop in Mound built a hiking trail along the Cascade Creek as a memorial to Douglas Shortley. Douglas had become an Eagle Scout under Carl's leadership and was killed in Vietnam. The trail begins with a bridge across the creek by cabin 10 and goes along the creek until it meets the Half-way Trail, which leads to the Cascade River.

The plaque reads as follows:
**"IN MEMORY OF EAGLE SCOUT DOUGLAS SHORTLEY**
**GAVE HIS LIFE IN THE SERVICE OF HIS COUNTRY**
**VIETNAM**
**1970."**

**127**

## The New Color Scheme, Redecorating and Other Projects

A very visible project during the late summer and fall of 1971 was the painting of the lodge. Just as the inside decor was in need of updating, the new exterior paint colors blended the lodge into the rustic setting. It involved a change in the color scheme of white and tan with green shutters, which had been in place for over thirty years, to a design involving two shades of brown with soft yellow trim on the second floor windows and roof lines. The restaurant had been painted in the new color scheme the previous year. Other changes included upgrading the game room in the basement of the lodge and adding some craft classes and evening activities during the summer months.

**The main lodge with the new external colors.**

During the winters of 1971-72 and 1972-73 redecorating the rooms in the main lodge became one of the main tasks. This included new furniture, carpeting, mattresses, etc. Regarding these changes in the lodge Mae wrote in the lodge's spring 1973 newsletter that "the better springs and mattresses (from the lodge) were going to the cabins to upgrade them a bit." This quote indirectly points out the great need to upgrade the interior of the cabins as well as the lodge while not having enough time and perhaps money to do everything at once. During the 1972-73 winters the remodeling included taking out the old steel radiators and installing baseboard hot water heaters in the guest rooms. With the new heaters each room now had its own thermostat to control the temperature. Although a major and necessary undertaking, Carl's knowledge and experience in the heating business was very valuable.

In the spring of 1972 Carl's attention returned again to hiking trail maintenance and development. This included rebuilding the stairway behind the restaurant, which is the first part of a popular trail leading to the river. In addition a hiking trail back to an abandoned homestead about three miles behind the lodge was developed. Later segments of this trail became part of the Pioneer Loop behind the lodge.

During the winter and spring of 1973 a new walk-in cooler and a room for cutting meat and for storage was added to the restaurant kitchen. This space was greatly appreciated by Bill Thomas the restaurant manager. Bill liked to purchase the meat for the restaurant in quarters and halves of animals and process the meat himself. With his butchering background this was a valuable asset to the operation. The additional storage and workspace was also much appreciated by the restaurant staff.

About this time, the growth of business in both the lodge and restaurant necessitated the drilling of a new well. The old artesian wells could no longer keep up with the demand for water. During the summer of 1973 a new 300 foot deep well was drilled, hitting a vein that proved to be an abundant source of water with minimal mineral content. The water is absolutely wonderful for drinking, cooking or bathing. Over the years guests have continued to remark on it's quality and excellent taste.

In addition to the actual drilling of the well, the project involved building a large underground concrete enclosure in the hill beyond the end of driveway from the main lodge. Then a water storage tank of 1,000 gallons was removed from the basement of the lodge and placed in the new enclosure. The final step involved burying a two-inch pipe to carry the water from the tank to the main lodge. This pipe had to be buried deep enough to keep the water from freezing in the winter. Along with the new supply of water a new domestic hot water heating system was added to the lodge plumbing, which made it extremely rare for the lodge to ever be short of hot water for showers.

## The El Ray Cafe is Purchased

Along with the growth and success of the business at Cascade Lodge came the opportunity to expand in a slightly different direction. On November 30, 1973 Mike and Sharon Rusten, Carl and Mae Odmark and Bill and Lois Thomas purchased the El Ray Cafe in Grand Marais. Mike and Sharon were the majority shareholders in the new venture. A day later they renamed the cafe the Blue Water Cafe. Bill Thomas was given the responsibility for establishing the menu and the overall supervision of the quality of the food and service at the new cafe and a new employee, Don Dewey, was hired to work with Bill as the on-site manager of the business. That winter the dining area of the cafe was completely remodeled.

## Staff Housing and a New House for the Odmarks

During 1973 the two dorm type rooms in the basement of the lodge were converted to staff rooms. Previously these rooms had provided economical ski season housing for youth groups and families. One room had two bunk beds and the other could sleep six people in three bunk beds. To compensate for this reduction in economical housing for skiers, a rotating bed arrangement in four units in the main lodge was instituted for the summer and winter months. In rooms 206 and 207 on the second floor of the lodge the double bed in each room was switched to a bunk bed for the winter. In addition, in apartments 1 and 2 on the first floor, (now numbered rooms 101 and 103) three sets of bunk beds were placed in each room for the winter instead of a double bed in apartment 1 and two single beds in apartment 2 for the summer.

During the winter months of 1973-74, the Odmarks built a house for themselves up the hill behind the main lodge and overlooking the creek. It was an unfinished prefab frame house that arrived in sections on a truck. After the house was assembled on the foundation Carl proceeded to finish the interior. The lower level of the house was designed as a walk-out basement with a separate entrance. This lower level space was furnished with five bunk beds and used for staff housing in the summer and rented to guests in the winter. The winter of 1973-74 also marked the last time that rooms 206 and 207 in the main lodge were rented out to guests.

**Carl and Mae's new house commonly called the Creek Chalet**. *Photo fall 1974.*

The new house on the property allowed Carl and Mae to distance themselves a bit from the 24 hour a day front desk responsibilities. These changes resulted in the hiring of Harold "Butch" and Rae Piepho on March 25, 1974 as host and hostess. The Piephos moved into Odmark's former apartment in the main lodge located behind the office. Butch had been a member of Carl's scout committee in Mound, Minnesota and the Piephos had also attended Calvary Memorial Church. By living in the apartment behind the front desk Butch and Rae became the primary people to check guests in and out in the early morning and in the late afternoons and evenings. They also answered the telephone and responded to front desk inquiries after the office staff had left for the day. Butch also assisted Carl on various maintenance tasks and projects and began to work on recruiting senior groups to come to the lodge. At that time Butch and Rae had three small children, so Rae's work at the lodge was less than full-time. With three children the Piephos needed more space than Carl and Mae had used, so room 101,[1] located off the living room by the fireplace, was switched back to being part of the apartment.

---

[1] The original room 101 was the room by the fireplace which is now used as an office.

## The Gas Shortage of 1974

In the 1974 spring newsletter to former guests, Mae Odmark reassured them that "we are completing our busiest winter yet, and so far our area seems to have an adequate supply of gas. Our [gas] station managers foresee no shortages this summer." As some may recall this was the first gas crisis or shortage in the U.S. since World War II. Within about a year prices for gasoline roughly doubled, stations cut their hours of operation and some closed on weekends. This situation was obviously a big concern to resort operators and to people making their vacation plans. Nobody wanted to make reservations somewhere and then not be able get there by car or get to their destination and find it difficult to buy enough gasoline to get back home. Anticipating a possible gasoline shortage, the lodge designed three and six-day bus packages for guests from the Twin Cities. These packages included daily events and side trips. Such plans were reminiscent of the emphasis on bus transportation for guests during the WW II years. Fortunately, the shortage never reached a critical stage and life went on pretty much as usual. Traveling to the lodge by bus remains an option for people who no longer drive a car or do not have access to a car. Many student employees who work seasonally at the lodge have also appreciated the availability of bus service. The bus company serving the lodge at this time is called Happy Times Tours, and operates out of Thunder Bay, Canada. As in the past, guests can be picked up and dropped off right at the lodge driveway.

**Fall View toward Lake Superior from Lookout Mountain.**

## Discovering Lookout Mountain

During one of Carl's first winters at the lodge, a neighbor, Ben Morgan, told him about an impressive outcropping in the hills behind the lodge. Carl was curious, so he decided to snowshoe up to the spot, which is about one-half mile behind the lodge. The place was about 1,260 feet above sea level and part of the Sawtooth Mountain Range. From the edge of the cliff Cascade Mountain, Lake Superior and the beautiful wooded Cascade Valley are visible. Carl was impressed and soon began calling the place Lookout Mountain, which over the years became the accepted name for the small mountain. Following this discovery, Carl and others on the staff at the lodge developed a new hiking trail to the mountain during the summer of 1974. A few years later a cross country ski trail to the site was developed and in more recent years the spot became part of the Superior Hiking Trail. During the 1980's an Adirondack shelter[2] and outhouse were added to the site. Today Lookout Mountain is a very popular hiking and cross country skiing destination.

[2] A three sided shelter with a roof.

**133**

**Cascade Mountain as seen from Lookout Mountain in the fall.**

## A Restaurant Cafe and Bakery in Two Harbors is Purchased

In the fall of 1974 lodge personnel expanded their business yet again with the purchase of Oscar's Cafe and Bakery in Two Harbors. Mike and Sharon were the majority owners and Carl and Mae Odmark, Bill and Lois Thomas, Butch and Rae Piepho and Pat and Sonia Wilson were minority owners with varying percentages of ownership. Sonia, another daughter of Carl and Mae Odmark, and her husband Pat moved to Two Harbors from the Minneapolis area and became the managers of the restaurant. The name of the restaurant was changed to The Harbor House Restaurant.

## Other Additions and Improvements at the Lodge

By March of 1976 a two-bedroom apartment was being added to the back of the motel building. It was originally intended for staff housing. At the same time the entire motel was winterized allowing for year-round rental of the three motel units. By the winter of 1978-79 the new apartment was permanently added to the guest rental options. This became the first truly two-bedroom rental unit at the lodge.

**The addition to the back of the motel. A two-bedroom apartment called 5D.**

Other improvements were also made at the lodge during the winter and spring of 1976. One was the replacement of the gas heaters in the cabins with electric heaters. The new heaters were sized to heat the cabins in the winter and were considered safer than the old gas space heaters. Another improvement was the remodeling of the rest rooms in the restaurant and some improvement made to lodge bathrooms.

**135**

## The Promotion of Cross Country Skiing

During the early 1970's cross country skiing began to attract some enthusiasts in Minnesota. By the winter of 1972 Carl Odmark saw the potential for developing ski trails at the lodge and started to promote the sport. The first mention of cross country skiing in the promotional literature of the lodge is the following statement in the 1972-73 winter rate card: "Make Cascade your headquarters for downhill and cross country skiing, snowshoeing, snowmobiling, winter photography, bird and wildlife watching. Trails begin at lodge." The first trail used by skiers at the lodge was the old logging road behind the lodge that was shared with snowmobilers. Part of this road became the east side of the current Pioneer Loop Trail. During the summer and fall of 1975 Butch Piepho cleared a trail on the west side of what became known as the Pioneer Loop. Prior to the 1975-76 winter Carl and Butch hired Larry Schutte, a local man, to make a track setter for the lodge, which could be pulled behind Carl's snowmobile. In the 1975-76 winter rate card the lodge advertised groomed cross country trails and snowshoes for rent. This was the beginning of groomed cross country ski trails at the lodge. During the next summer and fall (1976), Butch Piepho and Dallas Smith, another lodge employee, developed a cross country ski trail to Deeryard Lake and the former site of the Cascade Fire Tower in the Deeryard area. The estimated distance of the new trail system was about twenty-five miles. In an effort to get more guests out on skis the lodge purchased a supply of cross country skis, boots and poles to rent to guests during the 1976-77 winter season. With the lodge's emerging interest in cross country skiing, Carl Odmark was pleased to see Cascade River State Park hire a year around manager who was interested in the sport.

The new manager, Paul Sundberg, began working at the park on August 8, 1976. Prior to this time the park was closed in the winter and the manager's position was a nine month job. Paul's previous position was assistant manager at the Savanna Portage State Park located near McGregor, Minnesota, where he had developed sixteen miles of cross country trails and had observed the growing popularity of cross country skiing. Coming with the mandate to develop winter activities at the park, combined with his interest and previous experience in developing cross country trails, it was natural for Paul to immediately begin to develop trails in the park. As a means of getting going on the trails, he also borrowed a bulldozer from another park and roughed out the trails between Cascade River and Cascade Creek and made an access trail on the west side of Cascade Creek behind the lodge for a connection to the road leading to the Pioneer Trail. He also developed some trails in the park east of the river, a winter parking area in the park and insulated a park shelter for skiers to use.

In the fall of 1979 the lodge purchased a new Ski-Doo Alpine, double tracked snowmobile for grooming the trails. The Alpine was a powerful snowmobile designed for pulling groomers and heavy sleds. This made grooming much easier and improved the quality of the grooming. During the 1980's the development of the trail system continued to spread along the shore from the Cascade area west to Temperance River State Park and east to the Bally Creek Area. The development of the ski trails at the lodge and park marked the beginning of the promotion of cross country skiing at resorts and parks along the shore of Lake Superior.

**The Ski-Doo Alpine snowmobile with a trail leveling apparatus made by Butch and Carl. Note how narrow the trail is behind the equipment.**

## A New Septic System

As the lodge and restaurant business grew and as sanitation codes changed, the need for a new septic system emerged during the mid 1970's.

Compounding the problem of meeting this need was the fact that the lodge had very little land that was acceptable for an effluent drain field. Fortunately, excellent soil for such a purpose was available adjacent to the lodge on state property under the power line. After months of negotiations, a lease was arranged between the lodge and the Minnesota Department of Natural Resources, which gave Cascade Lodge the right to build a drain field under the power line. Construction began in the spring of 1977. The end result was a wonderful example of cooperation between a state agency and a private business. It is also a great example of a practical use of land on a power line right-of- way. In order to pump the effluent up to the new drain field, three pump stations had to be installed at intervals on the hill leading to the drain field. The system worked well and allowed for continued growth of the business. The drain field was significantly enlarged in 1998. By the year 2000 the baffle in the old holding tank by the main lodge had broken and the tile sewer pipe to the tank from the lodge needed to be replaced. Because of the increased occupancy at the lodge and the need to meet new sanitation codes, it was necessary to replace the one tank with three larger tanks. This required blasting ledge rock up to seven feet deep in spots in order to get the tanks deep enough into the ground. This was a costly project which should meet the needs of the lodge for many years.

## The Winterizing of Three Log Cabins

During the winter of 1978-79 attention was turned to the winterizing and remodeling of the three log cabins along the main driveway, beginning with cabin 3. To winterize the log cabin, a new foundation was put underneath the cabin, an insulated roof was built on top of the existing roof and the water supply line was buried as deep as possible and then insulated so that the water wouldn't freeze in the winter. In place of new windows or storm windows, plastic sheeting was put over the windows in the winter to help keep the cabins warm. The remodeling of the cabin involved building a new bathroom, a new interior wall, new carpeting, curtains, etc. By summer the cabin was finished. The winterizing of this cabin meant that the lodge now had one cabin that could be rented throughout the entire year. During the next winter cabin 2 was winterized and remodeled in a similar manner and during the winter of 1979-80 cabin 1 was given the same treatment. By undertaking these projects the lodge was increasing it's winter rental capacity and continuing the process of becoming a year around resort.

**138**

**Cabins 1, 2 & 3 are winterized. Notice plastic on windows**

## Carl and Mae Decide to Retire

By August of 1980 Carl and Mae had reached what Mae wrote in their 1980 Christmas letter as the "Magic Age of 65." They decided to retire at the end of the year and move into a home they had been building four miles away from the lodge. Mike and Sharon had known for sometime that this day was coming and had begun to consider their options regarding the future management of the lodge and whether or not they should sell the resort. Partly due to the fact that the Morning Star Greeting Company that they had founded was taking a lot of their time, they decided to sell the lodge. They knew I had been looking into the possibility of buying a resort and were aware that I held values similar to theirs. Mid-winter of 1979-80 they contacted me and asked if I had any interest in buying the lodge. After approximately a year and one-half of conversations and negotiations, Laurene and I purchased the lodge and the Blue Water Cafe as the principal owners on July 29, 1981. Thus began a new chapter in the history of Cascade Lodge.

**Back and front of the 1980 summer rate card.**

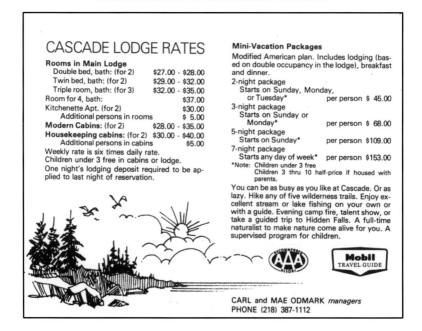

## CASCADE LODGE RATES

**Rooms in Main Lodge**

| | |
|---|---|
| Double bed, bath: (for 2) | $27.00 - $28.00 |
| Twin bed, bath: (for 2) | $29.00 - $32.00 |
| Triple room, bath: (for 3) | $32.00 - $35.00 |
| Room for 4, bath: | $37.00 |
| Kitchenette Apt. (for 2) | $30.00 |
| Additional persons in rooms | $ 5.00 |
| **Modern Cabins:** (for 2) | $28.00 - $35.00 |
| **Housekeeping cabins:** (for 2) | $30.00 - $40.00 |
| Additional persons in cabins | $5.00 |

Weekly rate is six times daily rate.
Children under 3 free in cabins or lodge.
One night's lodging deposit required to be applied to last night of reservation.

**Mini-Vacation Packages**
Modified American plan. Includes lodging (based on double occupancy in the lodge), breakfast and dinner.

2-night package
Starts on Sunday, Monday,
or Tuesday*     per person $ 45.00
3-night package
Starts on Sunday or
Monday*     per person $ 68.00
5-night package
Starts on Sunday*     per person $109.00
7-night package
Starts any day of week*     per person $153.00
*Note: Children under 3 free
Children 3 thru 10 half-price if housed with parents.

You can be as busy as you like at Cascade. Or as lazy. Hike any of five wilderness trails. Enjoy excellent stream or lake fishing on your own or with a guide. Evening camp fire, talent show, or take a guided trip to Hidden Falls. A full-time naturalist to make nature come alive for you. A supervised program for children.

CARL and MAE ODMARK *managers*
PHONE (218) 387-1112

**Inside panels of 1980 summer rate card.**

The first seasonal four-color brochure for the lodge. A separate summer and winter brochure was used starting in 1971. The quality of the color and design was widely recognized. Back and front panels.

Morning comes clear and cool to
the North Shore. The early sun stretches across
the watery horizon of Superior like a
waking cat, rubbing its warmth against the
dense, dark Cascade Forest. What a way
to start a day!
And what a day it's going to be.
Because you're at Cascade Lodge. Nine miles
east of the Lutsen resort area, nine miles
west of Grand Marais. And about as close to
heaven as you can get on this earth.

**Inside first fold of the 1971 brochure.**

What's your pleasure? Hiking? Well, you can just walk out the door of your cabin or the lodge and take any one of several trails through the virgin forest of evergreens and birch. The scenery is positively breathtaking and the birds, deer and other wildlife are plentiful.

Later, you can hunt for agates along the lake shore. You might even find a treasured Thomsonite. This is the only place in the country you can find one.

If camping, canoeing or fishing is your thing, you couldn't find a better base than Cascade.

Or if you like to golf or ride horses, these facilities are just a few miles down the road.

We're a friendly place, with lots of games and crafts and planned activities for children — of all ages! In the evening back at the lodge you'll always find friendly Christian fellowship.

And when you get hungry, have we got a treat for you: great food in the true North Country tradition.

So whatever your vacation pleasure, come stay with us awhile — a day, a week, as long as you can. We should warn you though, it won't be easy to leave.

**Inside left panels of 1971 brochure. The horses were from a stable away from the lodge.**

**Inside right panels of 1971 brochure.**

# *The Early Glader Years 1981-1989*

# Chapter IX

## Career Changes for the Gladers

In mid-summer, on July 29, 1981, life changed for my wife and me, as we became the principal owners and general partners of a partnership called Cascade Lodge Associates. I remember it well. I had driven up the day before with our youngest daughter Mary. My wife, Laurene, and Tom, our youngest son, flew up in a small plane with our attorney the day of the closing. Our two older children remained at their summer jobs in the Twin Cities and Seattle. The Rustens, and Laurene and I, and our attorneys met in the Grand Marais State Bank conference room for many hours that day reviewing and signing documents related to the sale. While Laurene and I were busy with the closing, Tom, who was about to enter the 10th grade and Mary, who was going into 7th grade, roamed around in what to them was the strange, new town of Grand Marais. Neither one had lived in a small town before. At the end of the day Laurene and Mary flew back to St. Paul to start the packing of our household goods, while Tom and I stayed in what was to become our new home at the lodge. It was the house the Odmarks had built in 1973 & 1974.

## Some Background about the Gladers

Because we have been asked so many times about what we did before we bought the lodge and how it came to be that we purchased the business, I will try to briefly answer these questions at the beginning of this chapter. Prior to purchasing the lodge I had been for twenty years a professor of physical education and a coach at Bethel College in St. Paul. Laurene had been a part-time nurse and nursing supervisor at Midway Hospital in St. Paul for about the same number of years.

My interest in owning a resort began the summer between my sophomore and junior years in college. At the time, I was transferring from Bethel College in St. Paul to Wheaton College in Illinois for my junior and senior years, where I could get a teaching major in physical education. When my friends heard that I was transferring to Wheaton and that I was interested in working in a Bible Camp for the summer, someone suggested that I ask to work with Gil Dodds at Word of Life Camp, a non-denominational camp in New York State. Gil Dodds, who had broken the world indoor mile record and outdoor American mile record in 1944, was the track coach at Wheaton College at the time. Working with Coach Dodds sounded like a great idea, so I wrote to him and the camp and got the job as Gil's assistant and as a counselor for the summer. It turned out to be a great experience on an island in upstate New York.

Near the end of that summer, the Word of Life organization purchased a resort on the mainland from where we embarked for the island. The resort was to be a place for families, whereas the island camp was primarily for junior high through college age guests. I thought the purchase of the resort was a great idea and it prompted me to begin dreaming about the possibilities of someday purchasing such a resort as a commercial business. During the next three summers I worked in various camps as preparation for a career in teaching and camping. However, the entrepreneurial spirit kept popping up in my mind after I graduated. During my two years in the Army I found myself thinking quite often about buying a resort or private camp. I was discharged from the U.S. Army in December of 1958 and returned to graduate school at the University of Minnesota during the winter and spring. During the spring of 1959 Laurene and I made our first visit to a resort that was for sale.

My summers for the next eleven years found me immersed in graduate school work followed by a few years working on writing projects and tasks associated with my position at Bethel College. The possibility of working in a YMCA or a Bible camp remained an interest, but it was definitely on the back burner during those years. By about 1976 the dream of buying a resort began to emerge more prominently again in my thinking. Consequently, I started looking at advertisements for resorts and began to wonder if it was a direction we should pursue. I had been at Bethel fifteen years, had finished my Ph.D. degree, was in my early forties and was a little restless.

As we looked at resorts we began to ask ourselves questions such as: How much do resorts cost? What could we afford? Did we want a small resort that we could operate in the summer while I continued teaching during the school year? Should we go into partnership with someone? And what type of resort was the best "fit" for us? After looking at several resorts around the state, we became primarily interested in the possibility of buying a year-round resort because we thought it would be easier to pay for a resort that had some income throughout the year. It was probably a good thing that we didn't fully realize the expenses that go with a year-round resort. We also concluded that for us the resort needed to be near an alpine ski area because we enjoyed

**146**

skiing and felt that close proximity to a downhill ski operation would be helpful to a resort that was open all year. With these parameters emerging, I marked on maps all the ski areas in Minnesota and Wisconsin and continued to look at resorts.

## Gene, Carl and Mae Meet Again

In 1973 or 1974 we had taken one of our children to spend a week at Mink Lake Camp on the Gunflint Trail. On the way home from the camp I decided to stop and say hello to Carl and Mae Odmark, whom I had not seen for years. I didn't know Carl and Mae very well at the time, even though Mae is my cousin and Carl had grown up on a farm near our farm on a small country road east of Cambridge, Minnesota. During our visit I learned that Carl had just replaced the old cast iron radiators in the lodge with new baseboard heaters. I became interested in the heaters because Laurene and I had recently purchased an old house on Lake Owasso in Shoreview, Minnesota, which needed additional radiators in the upstairs. Carl agreed to sell us about four of the cast iron heaters which we subsequently installed in our house.

The primary reason I didn't know Carl and Mae very well was because they were both about nineteen years older than I was and they didn't live near my home after I was a baby. Nevertheless, our lives have intertwined over the years in some interesting ways that relate to the history of Cascade Lodge.

My mother and Mae's mother were sisters. Over the years my mother had kept in contact with her sister and her niece Mae. After Mae graduated from a one-year teacher training program at St. Cloud Teachers College[1] in 1932, the school board of the little one room country school where my older siblings attended hired Mae to be the teacher. I believe my father was on the school board at the time. I eventually attended the same school for four years. Mae came to board in our house for three years while school was in session. During this time Carl Odmark was a young man whose family owned a farm one-half mile away and he and Mae became friends. At the end of Mae's second year of teaching, Carl and Mae were out on a date and when they came back to our house, my mother had just given birth to me. Carl and Mae related that story to me for the first time after we had purchased the lodge. After another year of teaching in our one- room school and staying in what was becoming a crowded house, Mae left and took another teaching job closer to her home in Zimmerman, Minnesota. About the same time Carl took

---

[1] Later became St. Cloud State College and now St. Cloud State University.

a job in the Minneapolis metro area. He and Mae continued their courtship and four years later they married. As I grew up I would occasionally see them at a family picnic or at our church, since the Odmarks and my family attended the same Baptist church.

During the summer of 1978, Laurene and I were again on the North Shore. This time we were looking at a resort for sale on the Gunflint Trail. On the way home we stopped in again to say hello to Mae and Carl. I also wanted to ask them what they thought of my dream of buying a resort. Carl indicated that he was very glad to be in the resort business and encouraged me to pursue the idea. At that time I learned that it was actually their daughter, Sharon, and her husband, Michael Rusten, who legally owned the lodge.

Our interests at the time were in resorts on smaller lakes in contrast to a large lake like Superior. About this time we had become interested in a resort in Wisconsin, which we did not have enough money to purchase alone. So I contacted Mike Rusten to see if he would be interested in investing with us in another resort. He informed me that he was not interested at that time; however, that is how we initially met each other.

## Cascade Lodge and the Blue Water Cafe are Purchased

By early February of 1980 Laurene and I decided to discontinue our efforts to purchase the resort in Wisconsin and put on hold our plans to buy a resort. A short time later, Mike Rusten called me and informed me that Carl and Mae were going to retire and that he and Sharon had decided to sell the lodge. He then asked if I would be interested in purchasing the lodge. This conversation was the beginning of about one and one-half years of discussions and negotiations.

To help facilitate the negotiation process, Mike and I hired a realtor as a mutual consultant. As our negotiations proceeded Laurene and I engaged an accountant and an attorney who set up a partnership for us with Laurene and myself as the General Partners and other possible investors as limited partners. Since Laurene and I did not have enough money for the down payment we began to look for other investors. Friends of ours, Dr. and Mrs. Lowry Fredrickson, became our first partners. Lowry was a psychology professor at Coe College in Iowa and his wife, Mary, was a nurse. Mike then gave bonuses to Butch and Rae Piepho, and Bill and Lois Thomas, which they agreed to invest in the lodge. Then the realtor who was our consultant

**148**

also agreed to make a modest investment. For the final portion of the down payment, the Grand Marais State Bank, of which Richard Anderson was president at the time, agreed to loan us $75,000.00 with the Blue Water Cafe as collateral. Thus the necessary money for the down payment came together and Laurene and I consummated the purchase in the middle of the summer. During the 1980's Laurene and I purchased the interests of everyone except the Fredricksons. In 1995 we changed the ownership structure from a partnership to a corporation and a short time later purchased the Fredrickson's stock.

The Blue Water Cafe as it appeared in 1981.

## Ownership Transition in the Middle of the Summer

Taking over a resort business at the height of its busy season is probably not the ideal time to change ownership, but the arrangement worked well for us. We had insisted as part of the purchase arrangement that all the key employees remain on the job at least through the first summer. This proved to be a very good decision, because it allowed us to gradually make the transition into the business. Butch had been the acting manager of the lodge for about six months, since Carl and Mae had retired. Bill Thomas was the manager of both the Blue Water Cafe and the lodge restaurant, Bernice Makila was

**149**

the head housekeeper and night clerk, Janice Clark was the head cook at the lodge restaurant and Rita Bodine was the bookkeeper. Their experience and leadership helped effect a smooth transition. It was comforting for us to know that Carl and Mae were nearby in their new home, if we needed some help or advice.

As a professor with tenure and twenty years of experience at Bethel College I was given a three-year leave of absence as we tried out the resort business. The leave of absence was a type of safety net for us as we changed careers. We initially rented out our house in Shoreview, just in case we wanted to return to the Twin Cities. Laurene, Mary and Tom moved up in August just before school started. Our older son and daughter were away at college.

The first year of ownership found us adjusting to our new home and occupation. In taking over the business at the end of July we had the benefit of the income from the busy months of August and September. This was helpful as we moved into the slow period between late October and Christmas. My background of growing up on a farm, working in camps and having been chairman of a physical education department and an athletic director proved to be helpful. Similarly, Laurene's background in nursing and supervision of nurses was helpful. However, neither of us had ever operated a cash register. During our first year we concentrated on doing essential repairs, maintenance projects, learning about the seasonal variations, hiring seasonal help, learning about the tourism associations in the area and state, trying to understand the income and expense cycles, and in general learning as much as we could about the business and the resort industry.

## Our First Maintenance Project

Our first maintenance project of some significance was the painting of the main lodge during August of 1981. A friend of ours, who was a teacher and ran a painting business in the summer, took on the task for us. He hired several high school kids, some of them friends of our family, to help him. They slept in sleeping bags on the floor of our house and got the job done before Laurene moved up with the furniture. Another of the physical improvements that we undertook the first year and one-half was to strip the paint off the woodwork in some of the main lodge rooms. The wood had been painted years ago and we wanted to restore the beauty of the wood trim around the windows and doors. One or two rooms were done in the slow time of April and early May in 1982 and again in the fall during November.

**150**

## The Transition to the Use of Computers

As I look back on the years of our ownership since 1981, perhaps the most important change has been the transition to the use of computers in conducting business by us and by virtually everyone we do business with. It wasn't that either Laurene or I knew anything about computers in 1981; it was just that times were changing and desktop computers were beginning to emerge as standard office equipment. We decided early on to try to adjust to the new technology.

When we purchased the lodge, the office equipment consisted of a cash register, a couple of calculators, an old electric typewriter, two safes, a little postage machine that didn't work and a thermo fax copy machine. This type of copier used a roll of waxy paper for making copies. Many of the daily business tasks were manually executed. All the checks for the lodge and Blue Water Cafe payrolls and bills were written by hand. For the payroll this meant calculating the employee hours and rate of pay by hand, and locating on a chart the amount to deduct for federal and state income tax and social security taxes. I soon began to look for a payroll service to help us. From an employee at the Grand Marais State Bank I found out that First Bank-Duluth had a payroll service. I contacted them and by November of 1981 our payroll was computerized. With the computerized payroll we not only received more complete individual payroll records, but a detailed breakdown of labor costs by job categories and departments.

As we approached our first Christmas at Cascade we wanted to continue the lodge's tradition of mailing a greeting to former guests. In previous years the letters had all been addressed by hand so we followed the same procedure and learned that it was a huge task. For the 1982 Christmas letter we contracted with a local lady, who was developing a computer business, to help us. We gave her a list of names and had her put them on her computer so she could personalize the letters and address the envelopes for us. Because of our inexperience with computers we didn't realize how much time and work it would take to put all the names into a database. Nevertheless, this was our second effort to incorporate computer technology into the business. By the spring of 1983 we realized that we "really" needed to either buy a new typewriter or "buy one of those new computers." Today this seems like it should have been an easy decision, but it wasn't then. The IBM Selectric typewriter still looked pretty good to us. We consulted with Laurene's brother

**151**

Herbert Jacobson, who had an electrical engineering degree and a master's degree in computer science. Even he wasn't instantly sure what we should do, but he finally suggested that we buy one of the new computers. So, by the summer of 1983 we had a new Epson computer, with a ten-megabit external hard drive and a new daisy wheel printer. The operating system used by Epson was called CPM. This was before the DOS system began to dominate the computer industry. Unfortunately, buying the CPM system was the wrong choice, and we had to convert everything to DOS by about 1985. Nevertheless, the move got us into the computer age and we began the process of learning how to use computers. There were many days and evenings during those years in which I spent many hours studying computer manuals and learning how to use the computer by trial and error. During the early 1980's computers were not very user friendly and it was not unusual for a program to have a glitch that the manual did not tell you about. I'm sure my wife wondered at times if this move toward using a computer was worth it. I kept convincing her that it was the right thing to do in the long run, even though I too had my doubts at times. Fortunately, it wasn't long before we were both convinced that we had made the right decision.

For about three years the entire office staff shared our one computer and the old typewriter. During these early years of using a computer I also found myself teaching new employees and college students who worked for us in the office during the summers how to use the computer. Years later, I tended to be the one asking the college students and new employees how to do things on the computer. Since 1983 it has been a gradual, continuous transition into the use of computer technology. This transition has involved buying more and faster computers, networking our computers, going from black and white monitors to larger color monitors, learning to use spreadsheets, databases, graphics, and the use of the Internet. We now use computers in virtually every aspect of the lodge business from processing orders and cashiering in the restaurant to a computerized reservation system in the lodge. The evolving use of computers during the past twenty years, has certainly changed many business procedures at Cascade Lodge. Our own evolution into the use of computers is a microcosm of how computers have changed every aspect of business, government, medicine, education and life in general during the past twenty years.

It is also interesting to reflect on our efforts to upgrade our copy machine in the mid-1980's to a copier that used regular (non-waxy) paper and the purchase of our first fax machine in 1991. All these decisions seem minor now, but at the time they were fairly major and involved equipment we had gotten along without over the years.

A beautiful fall picture of the lodge taken by a guest.

## A Growing Kinship with the Rustens and Odmarks

In taking over the lodge ownership and management from the Rustens and Odmarks I felt a growing kinship with them. They had done so much during their twelve years of ownership and management to winterize and update the lodge. I often felt that we were just picking up the "hammer and saw," where they had left it. Whether it was literally the "hammer and saw" or the continuous need to redecorate or upgrade furnishings and equipment, the feelings were the same. We were just continuing down a common path of change and growth as circumstances, times and money allowed. In addition, I have often reflected on the common backgrounds of Carl, Mae and myself. It seems providential that our paths crossed at Cascade Lodge some forty years after Mae came to live in my family's house on the farm.

In our first lodge Christmas letter to former guests we tried to express our desire to continue to operate the lodge with much of the same style that the Odmarks and Rustens had exhibited. We wrote as follows:

"As the new managers and principal owners of the lodge it is our desire to continue to operate the business with the same spirit as in the past. We hope that the lodge and the areas surrounding it will always be a place where guests can relax, have fun, be refreshed and be drawn closer to God. We hope you will come again and 'stay awhile'."

About this same time we made a welcome folder to give to guests when they arrived. In this folder was an insert with some seasonal information and pockets where various inserts such as maps, activity announcements and coupons could be put. In the brief welcome message on the front page of the insert we wrote the following which says a lot about our goals and philosophy at the lodge.

## "Welcome to Cascade Lodge

"We are very glad that you have chosen to spend some time here. Our facilities are here for your convenience and our staff is here to serve you.

"While you are here, we want you to have the option of having many things to do. However, we do encourage you to also be still and quiet at times in order to contemplate on the beauty and wonder of God's creation all around you.

"If we can be of additional service to you please do not hesitate to ask. We would also welcome any suggestions you may have for improving our facilities and services.

"When it is time for you to leave we hope you will have enjoyed some exercise, good meals and fellowship. In addition, we hope you will be physically, emotionally and spiritually renewed. We also hope that you will be eager to return."

The statement has been used for about twenty years and is still given to every rental party when checking in at the lodge.

## Changes in the Telephone Service at the Lodge

In 1981 the lodge had six telephones. Two in the office, two in the restaurant, one in the apartment behind the office where Bernice Makila, the head housekeeper and night clerk, lived and one in our house. When the phone rang in the office, it also rang in our house, but we didn't immediately answer it, unless it appeared that no one at the office was able to answer the call. We soon learned to ignore the short rings of the telephone in our house, like one learns to ignore noise from cars, buses and trains that may go by one's house in a city. Personal calls for us were transferred from the office to our house.

In 1985 we added a regional toll free "800" telephone number. A few years later the toll free number coverage was expanded to operate throughout the United States and Canada. By this time, travelers were beginning to expect to use toll free numbers to make reservations. The addition of a toll free number resulted in more calls to answer and the need to hire more office staff to help answer the calls.

By 1989 we decided it was time to give top priority to upgrading the telephone system. This was a big decision because it involved purchasing a hotel system for about $11,000.00. The first phase of the installation involved adding additional phones to the office and putting phones in all lodge and motel rooms. Phones were not installed in the cabins because of the additional expense it would have entailed. In addition, some guests indicated that they did not want phones in the cabins. They said they had come here to get away from phones. Nevertheless, over the next few years phones were gradually added to all the cabins, including the staff cabins. Now everyone seems to appreciate the convenience of a phone in their unit. An emerging use for the phones is connecting to the Internet with laptop computers. Having a phone in the rooms is also significant today because most cell phones don't work at the lodge. This is a common problem along the North Shore because the hills and valleys interfere with the signal. In about 1984 the telephone company installed pay phones in the main lodge and outside the restaurant. In the year 1999 or 2000 they were removed because they were no longer profitable to the telephone company due the increased use of cell phones and 800 numbers and, to some extent, the installation of phones in our rooms.

## Changes in the Availability of Television

Much like the telephone system at the lodge, the television options were quite limited in 1981. There were a total of eight TV sets on the property: four color sets and four black and white sets. One was in the living room of the lodge, four in the motel units, one in a staff room in the basement of the lodge, one in the head housekeeper/night clerk's unit and one in the head cook's cabin. We brought with us our television set for our house and this brought the number of sets on the property to nine. The signals from the TV translators on the hill behind Grand Marais were primarily directed toward the city. In addition, the hills between the lodge and Grand Marais prevented any signals from the translators from being picked up at the lodge. Consequently, the only available signals for us came from towers about 105 miles away in Duluth. Because of the distance, quality of our TV sets, power of the signals and interference from the Sawtooth Mt. range, the quality of the TV picture usually left much to be desired. Choosing what channel to watch usually meant checking to see which station came in the best on a given day. The good news in terms of our own family was that the quality of the signal and the limited channel options pretty much automatically kept the amount of time our children spent watching TV to a minimum.

Regarding our guests, it was understood that if they wanted a TV in the room they should rent one of the motel units or come to the main lodge to watch a program. There was also a prevailing opinion among the staff that guests did not come up to resorts with log cabins to watch TV, but to get away from the TV and telephone. In fact, as we started to think about putting TV's in the units several guests specifically told us that we should never put them in the log cabins.

Nevertheless, it wasn't long before we started buying one or two new color TV's a year and placing them in units that did not have TV sets. We also started buying portable VCR machines and some videos which could be rented by guests. Video stores also emerged in Grand Marais during the 1980's. Over the years guests became more interested in having a television set in their unit; they appreciated the option of being able to see the news, sporting events and weather reports. Since cable TV has never been an option at the lodge, during the early 1990's we began to look into the possibility of purchasing a satellite dish. In September of 1995 Starlight Satellite Systems from Duluth was hired to install a ten-foot diameter mesh dish and the equipment necessary for receiving three satellite channels so all units with TV sets could independently select the channel they wanted to watch. The system also gave us the opportunity to adjust the dish to pick up other channels from the same or other satellites that may have been broadcasting a game or special event that someone wanted to watch. This upgrade cost approximately $11,000.00. At the same time TV sets were installed in three lodge rooms and some cabins. It wasn't until 1997 that television sets were installed in all units. Then, in September 2000, a small 18 inch dish was added to the system, which gave every unit one channel with a digital signal. The system also provided additional flexibility for switching to other channels for special events. At this time, the installation crew also re-located the old antenna for the four Duluth channels from the motel roof to a higher location on the new garage roof. A year later an additional channel was added to the system. Around this time new high quality television cable was buried between the receivers and several buildings on the property. Guests now had a choice of four local channels, three analog channels from the large dish and two digital channels from the small dish.

## The Lutsen-Tofte Tourism Association Emerges

When we purchased the lodge in 1981 a new tourism organization was emerging in the west end of Cook County. This organization eventually became known as the Lutsen-Tofte Tourism Association. The primary common interest that united the businesses along the lakeshore to form the association was the development and the marketing of the North Shore Mountain Ski Trail. By the winter of 1982-83 this trail made it possible to cross country ski from Cascade Lodge or the Cascade River State Park to the Temperance River State Park in Tofte. With the development of the North Shore Ski Trail, cross country skiing became more popular at Cascade Lodge, as well as at other resorts along the shore.

An additional cause for the emergence of the Lutsen-Tofte- Tourism Association was a growing feeling among resorters on the West End of the county that it was time to develop a new organization that could more effectively market the businesses along the shore than the Tip of the Arrowhead Association. Prior to this time the Tip of the Arrowhead Association, which was a county wide organization, was the main promotional organization for the area. For several years following the formation of the Lutsen-Tofte Tourism Association, The Tip of the Arrowhead Association became the umbrella organization with representatives from the Gunflint Trail Association, Grand Marais Chamber of Commerce, the Grand Portage Area and the Lutsen-Tofte Association. By about the mid 1990's, the umbrella organization commonly called the "Tip" folded. The folding of the "Tip" was a little disappointing to me because I had been on its board for several years and had been the association's president in1989-90. The "Tip" had provided a significant service to its members over the years, but times were changing, and as local area associations in the county became stronger the "Tip" got weaker.

## Cross Country Skier and Snowmobiler Trail Conflicts

As cross country skiing was becoming more popular in the county, there was some conflict between snowmobilers and skiers over the use of certain trails. This conflict was partly due to the fact that both sports were relatively new and the concept of multiple uses of trails sounded very good to many citizens involved with public trails. It wasn't long before people began to realize that the common use of trails by cross country skiers and snowmobilers resulted in ruined tracks for skiers, and even more important, a safety issue for everyone. Soon everyone understood this. These conflicts were resolved in the early eighties when separate networks of trails emerged for the two sports. The new local snowmobile trail systems included a separate trail to the lodge through the park.

**Cabin 11 after it was winterized in 1983. Plastic was used to cover the windows in the winter, until 1998 when new windows were installed.**

## Remodeling and Winterizing Projects

The spring of 1983 marked the beginning of some major remodeling at the lodge. We began with cabin 11, commonly referred to as the Honeymoon Cabin at the time, although now we consider all of the cabins to be Honeymoon Cabins. The cabin had been built on posts in the ground and was continuing to settle on the north end and we knew that something had to be done with this popular cabin. I consulted with Tim Hall, a local mason, about putting a new cement and concrete block foundation under the cabin. Although he confidently said he could do it, the answer didn't seem quite that simple to me, due to the big stone fireplace on the south end of the cabin. Nevertheless, Tim and his co-worker jacked up the sagging, north end of the cabin, dug a trench for the foundation and soon had a new foundation in place. Simultaneously, we tore down the old attached bathroom and built a larger, new bathroom. We also preserved the rustic interior of the original roof by following the same method of building a new insulated roof over the existing roof that Carl Odmark had used. The real challenge for making the cabin usable in the winter was getting water to the cabin without having it freeze and connecting

**159**

the cabin's old sewage system to the lodge system. The water supply and septic problems were solved by connecting each to the respective restaurant systems. The hillside between the restaurant and cabin 11 proved to be one of the few places on the lodge property with sandy soil and no rocks, which made it possible to bury the pipes deep enough to avoid freezing in the winter. The winterizing of the cabin allowed us to almost double the number of nights the cabin was rented each year.

During the same spring the first phase of remodeling the second floor of the Blue Water Cafe in Grand Marais, was undertaken. This job included a new roof on the cafe, new windows on the second floor, removal of an interior wall, and installing a new small kitchen and bathroom on the second floor. Thus the Upper Deck of the Blue Water Cafe emerged from an old upstairs apartment.

**Cabin 10 after remodeling in 1983. The deck in photo was added later.**

Following the successful remodeling of cabin 11 in the spring of 1983, we decided to remodel and winterize cabin 10 during the late fall of 1983. This building also required a new foundation, but there was no stone fireplace around which we had to maneuver. We gutted the interior of the existing cabin and by rearranging all the internal features we were able create a whole new view of the creek area from the cabin living room. The water supply and sewage connections were made to the pipes servicing the motel, which proved to be fairly easily done.

It has been our experience that most remodeling and construction projects have a few surprises. To allow for construction problems and surprises we always tried to leave plenty of time before taking the first reservation for a unit. For cabin 10 we had taken a reservation for December 30, 1983 thinking that we were allowing plenty of time to get the unit ready, but the project did not progress quite as fast as we anticipated. Consequently, there were a few long days finishing the remodeling and putting the furniture in place, but the cabin was ready on time.

We continued our remodeling and winterizing projects in the spring of 1984 by gutting and remodeling cabin 8. When cabin 8 was finished we did the same thing to cabin 9. These are the two small cabins on the property without a living room and fireplace.

**Cabin 8 after remodeling.**

**Cabin 9 with cabin 8 in the background.**

In December 8, 1984, we experienced the first retirement of a long-term employee. Mrs. Janis Clark, had been the head cook at the lodge since the early 1970's. Fortunately, Janis was willing to work two additional summers at the lodge after she retired. Janis lived in what is now called cabin 6, but she also had a home on Devils Track Lake. After Janis moved out of her cabin in the fall of 1985 we converted it into a guest cabin and rented it out for the first time on December 30, 1985. In June of 1986 we began remodeling the cabin. We did this in three phases because of our own cash limitations. Phase one involved remodeling the bedroom, kitchen and bathroom in the cabin. Phase two involved remodeling the living room, installing a fireplace and adding a deck in the spring of 1987. Phase three involved installing new windows in the front of the cabin and new carpet in the spring of 1988.

**Cabin 6 with the enlarged deck.**

Some years later the deck was enlarged. The remodeled cabin has a beautiful view of Lake Superior and has become a popular choice for guests. There were no major remodeling or building projects undertaken during 1985, but like every other year a variety of little improvements were made to the buildings, grounds and equipment.

## The Retirement of Bill and Lois Thomas

A big adjustment to the business came in the spring of 1986 when Bill and Lois Thomas retired. Bill had been the restaurant manager since 1970, and after the purchase of the Blue Water Cafe oversaw both operations. During the 1970's Lois had worked in the lodge office and during the 80's she worked primarily as a cashier at the Blue Water Cafe. Lois had osteoporosis, which slowed her down during the 1980's. Bill's shoes were especially hard to fill. He had developed an extensive menu with some very good cuts of meat. Bill also had a great capacity to remember the costs of large numbers of products. He was an excellent "hands on" manager who viewed with considerable skepticism our first computerized guest check printer that printed out the order for the cooks in the kitchen as well as a guest check for the customers. We were sad to see Bill and Lois leave the Blue Water Cafe and lodge and

**163**

wished them well as they began a new stage of their lives. Bill now lives in the Twin Ports area where two of his daughters also live. Lois passed away a few years ago.

After Bill retired we tried hiring separate managers for the lodge restaurant and the Blue Water Cafe. However, we rediscovered that one overall manager was the most cost effective method for operating the two establishments. Daniel Riddle was hired to work at the Blue Water Cafe in 1986 and from 1998 to 2004 he managed both restaurants.

### Fishermen's Picnic Queens

In 1987, as part of the Fishermen's Picnic festivities, our daughter Mary was selected as the North Shore Queen. The Fishermen's Picnic is an annual city festival that takes place the first weekend in August and celebrates Grand Marais' heritage as a fishing community. A coincidence relating to Mary's selection as the North Shore Queen is the fact that LaVerne Neudahl, the daughter of previous owners of the lodge was selected as the North Shore Queen in 1951. In 1989, Sarah Piepho, the daughter of Harold "Butch" Piepho who worked at the lodge was selected as the North Shore Queen.

**Mary Glader, North Shore Queen 1987.**

## Area Recreational Developments

As the year 1989 arrived recreational facilities for tourists were continuing to expand in the area. At the Lutsen Mt. Ski Area, access to Moose Mt. was available by the gondola in February. During the summer the new Superior National Golf Course in Lutsen was under construction and by fall the Superior Hiking Trail was completed between Grand Marais and Taconite Harbor. These were all major developments which benefited all the resorts along the shore.

We ended the decade of the 1980's with enthusiasm for the business and a sense of having accomplished many goals, but with dreams and plans for many additional projects.

**The 1990 summer rate card. The card now has three panels.**

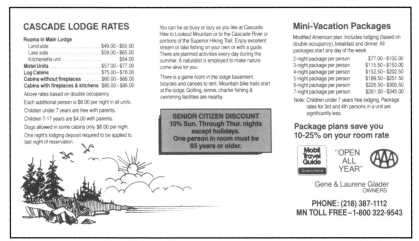

**Back and front panels of the newly designed, year around brochure.**
*Circa 1988.*

Start with the first warm days of spring, the steady trickle of melting snow and wild flowers poking their heads up through the woodland floor. Continue into the long warm summer days—hiking green woodland trails worn by those who have returned year after year.

Then relax with the sun reflecting on the water and rocks along the shores of Lake Superior. Inviting golden days of autumn offer unsurpassed color, crisp nights and firesides.

The scene changes—the serene quiet of the North Shore winter is broken by the sound of skis gliding through trees heavy with new fallen snow, beckoning you.

Whichever season you prefer—Cascade Lodge is there to welcome you.
*Come Stay Awhile*

**First inside panels in the new 1988 brochure.**

Cascade Lodge is a charming 1930's historic North Shore lodge nestled in the midst of the Cascade River State Park and featured in *Country Inns & America's Wonderful Little Hotels and Inns*. Comfortable lodge rooms, two large livingrooms, one with a grand stone fireplace, overlook Lake Superior. For those who prefer a quieter setting, there are log cabins with fireplaces – even the privacy of honeymoon cabins.

**Inside left panels in the 1988 brochure.**

From the first thing in the morning throughout the day, we are here to serve your appetites. Our distinctive North Shore restaurant, over-looking the lake, offers breakfast, lunch and dinner. Featuring local seafood and soup, salad bar and homebaked desserts.

Cascade Lodge on the North Shore is the place to vacation—renew your spirit—see things more clearly—and be able to return home refreshed. But, always ready to come back again and again.

Inside right panels in the 1988 brochure. Room on the left is 103 which was converted to a staff room in about year 2000.

# Chapter X

## New Cabins and Other Improvements

A time of important financial significance to the lodge was the year 1990. We had been working for at least two years to arrange financing for some additions and improvements at the lodge and the Blue Water Cafe. Finally with the help of First Bank- Duluth[1], the U. S. Small Business Administration and the Iron Range Resources and Rehabilitation Board (IRRRB) and the cooperation of Michael and Sharon Rusten we were able to put together a loan package. Prior to this time our primary financing was a Contract for Deed with the Rustens.

With the new loan we were able to build two new log cabins, numbers 7 and 12. There had been a cabin 7 on the property, to which we had made several improvements, but with the added experience of remodeling and winterizing other cabins, it seemed wise to tear down the old cabin 7 and replace it with a new one-bedroom unit. Cabin 12, our first two-bedroom log cabin, was a completely new unit and not a replacement cabin. In the midst of finalizing the designs for both cabins we began to realize the growing popularity of two person whirlpools in newly constructed motels and resorts so we decided to alter the plans to include whirlpools in the bathrooms. Both cabins also had kitchenettes, free standing fireplaces, decks and living rooms. Cabin 7 was made from eight inch machine rounded logs and cabin 12 was made with big "Englemann spruce" logs from Oregon and hand crafted by Mike Senty, a local log home builder. Cabin 7 was completed in the fall of 1990 and cabin 12 by Christmas. Immediately these units proved to be very popular.

---

[1] Now called the US Bank

**Cabin 7. First rented in the fall of 1990.**

**Cabin 12. First rented in December of 1990.**

172

All the other guest cabins at the lodge had previously been winterized. Of course the new cabins were also winterized. The one exception to the complete remodeling of all the cabins was the need to install new thermo pane windows in the original four log cabins. Prior to installation of the new windows in these cabins in 1998, each fall we would place plastic sheets on the outside of the windows to keep the heat in and the cold out during the winter.

The completion of the winterizing and remodeling of all cabins in 1990 was a significant milestone for the lodge. It was a very costly process that took twenty years and would be extremely expensive to do today. The process involved burying new water pipes, replacing old sewer pipes, installing new bathrooms and almost a total re-wiring for electricity, as well as the addition of insulation to the walls and ceilings of all cabins. Under most cabins new foundations were built and new windows were installed.

**The Blue Water Cafe with new signage and completed Upper Deck.**

With money from the new loan we were also able to remodel the lodge restaurant and the Blue Water Cafe. At the lodge restaurant this involved tearing out the interior walls and windows in the dining room, insulating the walls, installing new thermo-pane windows and then sheet rocking and paneling the interior walls. The restaurant building, built in 1946, was not designed for winter use, so no insulation had previously been placed in the walls or ceiling. However, windows did have storm windows. The large picture windows facing the lake had only single pane glass. The new windows and insulated walls made for a much more comfortable dining experience for guests and also reduced the cost of heating the building. At the Blue Water Cafe the dining area was enlarged, new bathrooms and a furnace installed, and a new stairway to the Upper Deck was built.

We also decided to stop allowing pets in the lodge rental units in 1990. The problems of dogs being left alone in cabins and barking, jumping on beds, frightening housekeepers finally came to a climax. The decision made some guests happy and disappointed others. People allergic to dog hair were probably the happiest.

## Changes Brought about by Bernice Makila's Retirement

As we moved into 1991 we experienced the retirement of another long-term employee. Bernice Makila, our head housekeeper and night clerk, decided to step down because of health problems. Bernice lived in the apartment behind the front desk where the Neudahls, Odmarks and Piephos had all lived. She had been with the lodge since 1978. Prior to Bernice's arrival at the lodge, the Piepho family had moved to a house they had purchased on the Caribou Trail.

**Bernice Makila working at the front desk.** *Spring 1982.*

In addition to her housekeeping and night clerk duties Bernice helped out at the front desk. In the early eighties she was responsible for answering the telephone and checking guests in and out from 9:00 P.M. to 8:00 am. During those days she would even take the reservation notebook to her bedroom and sometimes take a reservation late at night.

Her retirement obviously prompted some changes around the lodge. The most visible change was the remodeling of part of her apartment into a rental suite. With changes in staff responsibilities, we no longer felt the need to keep an apartment behind the office. A beautiful suite was made out of the living room, which had a stone fireplace and two picture windows, and the bedroom, which also had a picture window facing the lake. A closet and bathroom were remodeled into a new bathroom that included a two-person whirlpool.

The kitchen part of the apartment became necessary office space and a second bedroom behind the office became a bedroom for seasonal staff. The staff person who stayed in this room was usually the night clerk at the lodge.

## Activity and Naturalist Programs

Over the years the lodge has provided naturalist and activity programs for guests. For many years a naturalist/activity leader was hired to conduct guided hikes, show films or slide shows in the evenings, host campfires and lead other activities.

In the summer of 1992 a guided evening and day canoe trip was added to the activity options at the lodge. The evening trips involved driving up the Gunflint Trail to a landing on the Brule River and canoeing down the river a short distance to Northern Light Lake and back up the river. In addition to the enjoyment of canoeing, guests frequently saw some moose and other wild life on these trips.

The canoe program was started partly in response to the discontinuance of the staff talent show. From the mid 1970's through 1991 the lodge staff had put on a talent show for guests one night a week during the summer. During the process of hiring summer personnel preference was given to students that would enjoy performing in the show. However, as we approached the 1990s, interest in the talent show was waning both on the part of our staff and guests. In 1991, we were told by the State of Minnesota, Department of Labor, that

**175**

we had to pay students for both their practice and performance time. Up to this point it had been a voluntary opportunity for the staff. The state's view was that some employees probably felt obligated to perform and therefore we needed to pay them. There may have been some truth to this view and since it was not feasible to invest that much money into the talent show, we decided to discontinue it.

During recent years we have participated in a naturalist program run by the U.S. Forest Service in cooperation with the Lutsen-Tofte Tourism Association. Under this program various resorts host different programs throughout the week which are open to the public. Cascade Lodge has frequently hosted a campfire on Thursday nights and a guided hike on Saturday mornings as part of this program. Guests from all resorts are encouraged to go to whatever activity or program interests them, even though they may not be staying at the resort hosting a program. It has been a very good cooperative program.

## Highway Improvement During the 1990s

In the fall of 1992 driving to Cascade Lodge became safer and faster again for most people because the Highway I-35 bypass through Duluth along the lake was completed. A year earlier the first tunnel at Lafayette Bluff on the North Shore Drive was completed and in 1994 a second tunnel at Silver Cliff opened as an additional major highway improvement. Since 1994 additional sections of Highway 61 have been improved almost every year. The improvements most noticeable for travelers have been the elimination of some hazardous curves and the widening of the shoulders in many places. The accumulative effect of all the highway improvement has been quite dramatic. There is no doubt that each improvement in the highway has benefited the lodge and other businesses in Cook and Lake Counties. All the highway improvements over the years have made it easier for millions of people within a five-hour driving range to take mini vacations or extended vacations on the North Shore.

## Participation in Tourism Associations

As part of our management style we always placed a high value on involvement in professional and trade associations. Laurene and I felt it was important to learn from others in the industry and to contribute to the industry by being involved in appropriate associations. We have always felt that others in the resort industry are primarily our colleagues and to only a small extent our competitors. We have always felt that by working together we all benefit. This has been our experience with the Lutsen-Tofte Tourism Association, the Grand Marais Chamber of Commerce, the former Tip of the Arrowhead Association in Cook County, the Arrowhead Association, the Lake Superior North Shore Association and the Minnesota Resort Association. We have been members of all these associations and I have served on the board of most of them over the years. In 1989-90 I had the privilege of being the president of the local, county-wide, tourism organization called the Tip of the Arrowhead Association and in the fall of 1992 I had the privilege of being elected president of the Minnesota Resort Association. In 1993, when I was president, two of my colleagues from our small county also served as presidents of two other tourism associations. Dave Tuttle, from Bearskin Lodge, was president of the Cross Country Ski Areas Association, and Bruce Kerfoot, from Gunflint Lodge, was president of the National Association of Canoe Liveries and Outfitters. It was quite unusual for three people from a small, somewhat remote area, to be elected to lead three such organizations in the same year. I believe that all of us had a similar desire to serve and learn through our trade association involvement.

It is my understanding that Carl Odmark felt the same way as we did regarding involvement in tourism organizations. When he managed the lodge he was very involved in the local and regional tourist organizations. His belief in the importance of being involved in tourism organizations was evident when he took me to association meetings and introduced me to various folks after we had purchased the lodge This was a very nice gesture by Carl and helpful to me as a newcomer to the area.

**Three simultaneous association presidents from Cook County: Dave Tuttle of Bearskin Lodge, Bruce Kerfoot of Gunflint Lodge and Gene Glader of Cascade Lodge.** *Photo from Cook County News-Herald.*

**Gene Glader received the "Resorter of the Year" award in 1994 from the Minnesota Resort Association. Andy Kroneberger, a former Resort Association President and a recipient of the "Resorter of the Year" honor is giving the award to Gene. Laurene Glader is on the left.**
*Photo from Association Newsletter, Hospitality Focus.*

## Fire Safety and Fire

We have always welcomed safety suggestions by the State Fire Marshall and others. Following some fires at other resorts the Marshall suggested that a new centralized smoke and heat alarm system be installed in the public areas of the main building and sprinklers in the basement level of the building. These improvements were made in 1993. That same year it was also decided to make the main lodge a non-smoking building for health and safety reasons.

In spite of our concerns about safety and fire prevention we did lose an old storage building and small staff cabin to a fire in October of 1993. The fire apparently started after a newly hired housekeeper put some ashes from a fireplace into a wastebasket in the storage building. She apparently didn't realize that ashes could flame up even when they appeared to be out. Normally the ashes are put into a special container away from buildings. After the storage building was consumed by flames the fire spread to the nearby summer staff cabin. No one was living in the cabin at the time. Fortunately, the fire took place in the daytime. In recent years the little staff cabin was called the "Doll House," but had been guest cabin 4 when the Neudahls owned the resort. During Neudahl's years of ownership the storage building was the place where Minnie Neudahl and her staff did the laundry. In recent years the building was used primarily for storage of old restaurant equipment and supplies, and miscellaneous old furnishings. Fortunately the fire was confined to these two buildings and nothing of great value was lost. In fact, we had been considering tearing down the storage building. The fire was a sobering experience and a good reminder to be even more safety conscious.

**Storage Building fire on October 7, 1993.** *Photo by Jackie Meyers.*

**The fire is almost out. The storage building is gone, but the frame of the staff cabin is standing.** *Photo by Jackie Meyers.*

## A New Garage Storage Building is Built

A partial solution to the storage dilemma was the construction of a new garage near our house in 1994. The garage was fully insulated and was big enough to park a car, the lodge pickup, and several smaller machines such as snowmobiles or ATV's, snow blowers and lawnmowers inside, and still have space for a workbench. There was also a large storage attic above the garage level. The garage was built into a hill, which necessitated moving many yards of dirt. This dirt was used to level an area just west of the garage for a volleyball court and horseshoe pit. The long range plan for the space is to build a tennis court with a surface that could also be used for basketball and volleyball.

**New Garage built in 1994. Note large TV satellite dish beside the garage which was installed in 1995 and the small 18" dish on the garage, which was installed in 2000.**

The garage was a much needed facility at the lodge. This was especially true after the State Fire Marshall informed us that we could no longer park any machines or vehicles with gasoline motors in the garage under the lodge. At about this same time, we had begun to look for a golf car type vehicle for use by our housekeeping staff with the intent of parking it in the garage

**181**

under the lodge. The new fire code prompted us to purchase an electric golf car type vehicle, which we could park safely in the garage under the lodge. Butch Piepho built a storage box for the back of the vehicle that worked very well. The car proved to be an extremely valuable piece of equipment for the housekeeping staff with the increased number of cabins to clean year around. It surprised everyone on the staff to see how well it worked in the winter. After we had had the car for a few months, one of our housekeepers said to me, "You know, I think that car is saving us one person a day on the housekeeping crew." It truly was one of our better purchases. Our only regret was not buying one sooner.

**Housekeeping car with Claudia Bustamante, a student from Peru as the driver.**
*Photo January 2003.*

**Interior of cabin 2 with the new fireplace which was installed in 1994.**

## Cascade House Property Purchased

In the spring of 1994 a house on 17 1/2 acres of land two miles east of the lodge came up for sale. The house was in great need of repair and the four other buildings on the property were literally falling down. Another problem was the fact that dozens of components of various old cars and trucks were spread around the property. Laurene and I looked at the property, and in spite of all its negatives, decided to purchase the house and land. At the time we weren't sure if we should use the house for staff lodging or fix it up for guests. We immediately began cleaning up the property and repairing the house. We hired a man who hauled scrap metal and did demolition work to help us. He hauled away six semi-truck loads of junked car and truck parts and burned the out buildings for us. By winter we had finished remodeling the first floor of the house and decided to start renting it out to guests. We named it the Cascade House.

**The Cascade House at the time of purchase, 1994.**

Two years later, in 1996, a section of highway 61 that stretched in front of the house was rebuilt. The contractor asked if he could put the excess dirt from the project into the old gravel pits behind the house. We were very glad to have this fill and it improved the landscaping of the land immensely. The contractor also asked to use some of the land behind the house for a place to park his road building equipment and for crushing some gravel. We said that was fine also. In exchange for the use of our land the contractor blacktopped the driveway to the Cascade House and the restaurant driveway when his road building project was completed. By 1998 the house was completely remodeled and included a sauna and whirlpool in the basement.

**Cascade House after remodeling.**

**The entire parking lot of the restaurant was blacktopped in 1996. The covered handicapped ramp was added in 1992.**

## New Locks, Deadbolts and Enlarged Rooms

In 1995 the American Automobile Association (AAA) issued a new requirement for member properties. The requirement stated that deadbolts, which could be opened only with an emergency key from the outside, were to be installed in the doors of all units. To keep in good standing with the AAA and to provide added security for our guests, we changed all the locks and added deadbolts to all the exterior doors of all units. Now it is interesting to look back on the many years when the only key used for cabins was a simple skeleton key available at the time in many hardware stores.

About this same time we realized that some of the main lodge rooms were considered pretty small by new motel standards. Therefore, we began a process of combining two lodge rooms into one larger room with a new and larger bathroom. The first combined room was a combination of 201 and 205 into a new 201 in 1995. In 1996 we combined rooms 211 and 215 into a new 211, which included a two person whirlpool. In the year 2000 rooms 207 and 209 were combined into one room. All the new rooms have two queen beds.

## Upgrading the Outdoor Chapel

By 1995 the original log benches in the outdoor chapel were past the starting point of rotting. So, Dan Roberts and Tim Pennings undertook the task of making new benches and a pulpit for the chapel.[2] They used some of the leftover log pieces from the construction of cabin 12 and some half logs given to us by Mike Senty. They also grubbed out a big tree stump and relocated the log benches into a better layout. The new benches and layout have been a much appreciated improvements to the beautiful chapel setting. The Odmarks and Rustens had started a half hour chapel service on Sundays during the summer months back in the 1970's. We have continued the service during the months of July and August. In recent years it has been common to host one or two weddings in the chapel each summer.

**Wedding at the outdoor chapel in 2002.**

---

[2] Dan Roberts is a teacher who had worked at the lodge many years, from the time he was a student in college. Tim Pennings is a math professor at Hope College who had helped us at the lodge for a about three weeks each summer for several years.

**187**

## Family Members Return Home

In the spring of 1995 our youngest daughter Mary and her husband John Hay moved to the Lutsen area. Mary had worked in a wide variety of jobs at the lodge during her high school and college years so it was wonderful to have her return home and begin to work in the office and other areas at the lodge again. She managed the gift shop, was a group marketing representative and worked at the front desk. Mary now has three children and works only part-time at the lodge. When John arrived we needed a manager at the restaurant so John helped us out there for about two years during a management transition time. John then moved on to a full-time position at the local credit union.

The next spring our son Tom moved back to the area with his wife Carol and their first child. Tom worked at the Blue Water Cafe for the first six months and then joined the lodge office staff and became the marketing representative for the lodge. One of his first major assignments was to get us connected to the Internet and to develop a website for the lodge. This was done during 1997 and has had an impact on our business beyond our wildest early dreams. Carol took over the management of the gift shop and assisted with some bookkeeping tasks.

## The Purchase of Kassbohrer Piston Bully Groomers

The years of 1995 and 1996 were a milestone period in the development of the cross country ski trails at the lodge, as well as for the entire North Shore Mountain Ski Trail system. In the fall of 1995 the Lutsen-Tofte Tourism Association purchased an almost new Kassbohrer Piston Bully groomer to be used on the entire trail system. The cost of the used machine was approximately $93,000.00. The primary location for the groomer was at Bluefin Bay Resort and it was brought to Cascade Lodge as often as was practical. The purchase of the groomer prompted a major effort to widen all the ski trails so they could accommodate the groomer, although not all trails were adequately widened the first year. Consequently, it wasn't possible to drive the groomer to Cascade from Bluefin Bay, so the groomer had to be hauled on a trailer between the two resorts. The drivers for the groomer were provided by Bluefin Bay Resort, Cascade Lodge and Solbakken Resort.

The experience of the first year with the new groomer convinced association members that the quality of grooming and track setting with the Piston Bully machine was superior to that done by our older and smaller

**188**

groomers pulled by snowmobiles or other vehicles. We also realized that one machine could never adequately meet the grooming needs of the entire North Shore Mountain Ski Trail. The association members knew that the area trails were emerging as a first class trail system and no one wanted to compromise on quality. Within this framework, some of us began to work on proposals by which the association would purchase a second Piston Bully groomer. By late summer of 1996 a second, almost new groomer was located that cost about $120,000.00 and the association agreed to purchase it.

**Kassbohrer Pisten Bully groomer shared by Cascade Lodge and Solbakken Resort.**

The purchase was contingent upon a somewhat complicated lease agreement between the Lutsen-Tofte Tourism Association and Cascade Lodge and Solbakken for one machine and a similar agreement with Bluefin Bay for the other machine. The agreement designated Cascade Lodge as primarily responsible for grooming the trails close to the lodge, and the Deeryard Lake and Pioneer Trails. Solbakken was responsible for grooming from the west Cascade Park parking lot to the golf course at Lutsen. Bluefin Bay was to groom the trails from the Temperance River to the golf course. The agreement also committed the resorts to provide heated garages for the groomers. At Cascade we were mentally, but not financially, prepared to build a new garage if Solbakken Resort didn't do so. Early in the season we had tried to drive the groomer into our garage, but discovered that the groomer was just a little too high to clear the garage door opening, so we parked the groomer outside for a while. Then one day we needed to repair something on the rear of the groomer so I suggested to Butch Piepho, who was our operator, that he back it into our heated garage as far as possible. I thought we could then wrap a canvas around the front of the groomer and keep out some of the cold while we fixed the machine. To our surprise the top of the groomer was lower when we backed it in and came within a quarter of an inch of clearing the door frame. The difference in height was due to the fact that the cab on the front of the groomer leveled off when the machine was backed into the garage, in contrast to being at a slight upward angle when driven forward into the garage. Then we discovered that if we bent the metal guard for the light on the top of the cab, we could get the groomer completely in the garage. We did bend the metal guard down slightly and from then on the groomer was been parked in our heated garage saving both ourselves and Solbakken the expense of having to build a new garage. However, then our pickup truck had to be parked outside.

According to the lease agreement the three resorts received some reimbursement for grooming the trails and maintaining the machines. The association also accrued a debt owed to the three resorts for grooming and maintenance costs over the years under the terms of the agreement. The debts were paid off in 2003 by transferring the title of one groomer to Cascade Lodge and Solbakken Resort and the title of the other groomer to Bluefin Bay Resort. As part of the transfer arrangement the three resorts agreed to continue grooming the trails with the same machines under a new payment formula.

All the trails in the system were soon widened to accommodate the Piston Bully groomers. One of the features of the groomer that was especially helpful was the tiller which grinds up ice that sometime accumulates on trails. The trails commonly associated with Cascade Lodge, after approximately twenty-five years of development, have truly evolved to a very high quality. Butch Piepho, who worked at the lodge for twenty-six years, until he left for another opportunity in October of 2000, was one of the people who has done a lot of work on the trails over the years. Because the trails in our area are primarily on state and federal land we have received several thousands of dollars in grants from the county, state and federal governments as assistance in developing the trails. Most of the grant money was used to purchase and install culverts, hire heavy equipment to remove stumps and rocks, dig ditches and smooth out sections of the trails. Most of these grants had to be matched with money and labor from the lodge and volunteers or other grants.The North Star Ski Club in Minneapolis has been the most consistent organization in recruiting volunteers to help maintain the trails each year. As the quality of the ski trails have evolved they have also received more use during the non-winter months by people with other interests such as hiking, mountain biking, hunting and bird watching.

**The new Polaris Ranger ATV and North Star Ski Club volunteers working on clearing the cross country ski trails of branches in October 2002.**

## The Hiring of International Students

During the 1990s it became increasingly more difficult to hire enough help for various jobs around the resort. This was especially true during the months of September and October, which have become progressively busier over the years. Compounding the problem was the fact that most U.S. students needed to return to their schools and colleges in late August or early September. Another factor that added to the labor shortage in Cook County was the growth in the number and size of tourist-oriented businesses. Many of these businesses needed more help and yet the local population of working age people was not increasing in any significant way. In fact, the number of young people of high school age that usually met some of the summer labor needs, was declining. In addition, unemployment levels were low both nationally and in Minnesota during the 1990s. As a result most college age seasonal workers had summer job options closer to home.

The solution for us was to participate in exchange programs which helped to arrange employment for foreign college and university students. We were introduced to one program by our friends, Barney and Darcy Peet, who own three motels in Grand Marais. We phased into the program by hiring students, who worked for them in the morning as housekeepers, to work for us in the afternoon and evenings as waiters, waitresses and dishwashers. By the spring of 1995 we had begun to make our own arrangements for hiring most of the foreign students who worked for us. We have also continued to employ students who work for the Peets in the mornings. Most of the international students come through an organization entitled the Council on International Education Exchange. Between the Blue Water Cafe and the lodge we have been employing about 12 to 25 international students per year, either full-time or part-time. Under the various exchange programs, students can receive a work permit for up to four months. Some students have been able to return two or three times under the program. We hire primarily students who can stay and work until at least mid October so that we have help through the busy fall season. These students usually don't arrive until mid June or later.

Our year-round staff and some American college students were usually able to meet our help needs during late May and early June. The American staff was then available to help the international students, when they arrived, to adjust to their new situation and phase into their jobs. Then the combined new staff was usually well prepared for the busy months of July and August.

**192**

Most of the foreign students here for the summer or fall came from England, Ireland, Scotland, Spain, France, Lithuania, Latvia, Poland, Belarus, Russia, Guinea (Africa), Czech Republic, Slovakia and the Dominican Republic. For the winter season we usually hired between two and four students from the southern hemisphere who were on their summer vacation. These students came from countries such as Australia, Costa Rica, Peru and Brazil.

We also sponsored and/or employed six international students on internships for six to eighteen months each during the last few years. One of these students came from Lithuania, another from Ukraine and four came from Japan. These students had an interest in the hospitality business and wanted to work in an American resort. We employed them in both the restaurant and the lodge.

**A rest stop at the top of Lookout Mt. during a day of skiing with Miki Hasegawa, an intern from Japan. In the picture from left to right. Micah and Luke Glader, Tim and Barbie Glader, Victoria Glader, Laurene Glader and Miki.**

The student exchange program has been a great success. With only one or two exceptions, the students have been wonderful employees. All the students have wanted to improve their ability to speak, write and understand English. Students that cannot speak or understand much English usually begin working as housekeepers, dishwashers or in general maintenance. Students who speak more fluent English when they arrive usually start out as cashiers, hosts or servers in the restaurant. We try to provide extra opportunities for the international students, such as making sure that they get to Duluth occasionally, taking them to some special local events, local church services and other things they may want to do or see. Our staff has really enjoyed having the international students in our midst and our guests have enjoyed visiting with, and being served by international staff members. It has been a wonderful cultural experience for all of us. As a former college professor, it has been especially enjoyable for me to work with American and International college students during my years at the lodge.

### The July 5th Flood

The days of July 4 and 5, 1999 will long be remembered in Cook County. On July 4th between about 11:30 A.M. and 2 P.M. the upper Gunflint Trail and Boundary Waters Canoe Area Wilderness was hit by a severe windstorm. Millions of trees were blown down and considerable damage was done to property. Several people canoeing in the Boundary Waters were injured; but, amazingly, no one was killed. At the lodge we experienced no significant change in the weather and we knew nothing about the storm. In the evening when we went into Grand Marais to watch the fireworks, we noticed some emergency vehicles stopping traffic on the Gunflint Trail near the hospital and thought that there perhaps had been a motor vehicle accident up the trail. We continued driving toward the harbor to watch the fireworks and didn't learn until the next day that there had been a major storm up the trail. Communication was severely limited between those living up the trail and Grand Marais since power and telephone lines were down and trees were on the road. As the fireworks ended, a heavy rainfall began in Grand Marais, but as we neared the lodge the rain had almost ended.

About 2 A.M. on July 5th I was awakened by a phone call from some guests in cabin 2 telling me that there was water in their cabin. I was totally stumped as to how there could be water flowing into their cabin, but I told them I would come down and check it out. When I left the house the rain was just pouring down and as I started walking down the driveway the water was up to my ankles. When I arrived at cabin 2, I learned that the guests that called me had been in cabin 11 but had left it for the safety of cabin 2, where their friends were staying. The folks in cabin 11 had awakened in the night and had noticed that water was seeping into the cabin. Fortunately, they decided right away to gather their things and cross the creek by using the bridge and went to cabin 2. If they had delayed much longer they would not have been able to leave the cabin safely.

The creek continued to rise for another two to three hours until it reached about four feet in depth at the backside of cabin 11 as it flowed under and around the cabin. The bridge over the creek by cabin 10 was destroyed and floated down the creek, but somehow the bridge to cabin 11 survived.

**Flood scene at about 5 A.M. after the water had started to recede. Note part of the bridge which used to be by cabin 10 and other debris on the stone footbridge.**

A considerable amount of rock, trees and debris had washed down the creek. Some of the debris jammed up and formed a dam by the stone bridge between the lodge and restaurant, constricting the volume of water that could pass under the bridge. This contributed to the amount of water that was forced up over the creek bank and washed out a section of the restaurant parking lot. Between 2 A.M. and 5 A.M. the water flowing over the highway between

**Flood washing away the foundation of cabin 11 and part of its porch. The peak of flood water was about three feet higher around the cabin than in the above picture. Photo at about 8 A.M.**

the restaurant and the lodge sign was about a foot deep in places and traffic was stopped on the highway for two to three hours. By 4 AM, most, if not all, of our guests and staff were awake. At about 5 A.M. I called our son Tom in Grand Marais, to come and capture the flood on film. By 6 A.M. the rain had let up and the water started to recede. About 6:30 A.M. I called Irving Hansen, of Isak Hansen and Sons, (the same local contractor that had assisted Carl Odmark years earlier) and told him I had a problem and asked if he could bring a logging truck over and lift the debris out of the creek where it had formed a dam. Irving promptly sent a man and truck over to start working on the problem. If he had delayed, the damage to the parking lot would have been much greater.

By about 8 A.M. things seemed to be under control and we began picking up one stick at a time in our effort to clean up the area. Irving Hansen then provided a dozer, excavator and trucks for about three days to repair the driveway, clean out the rocks, trees and debris from the creek and rebuild the edges of the creek. Later Irving provided a crew of craftsmen to reconstruct a foundation under the cabin, build a retaining wall for the creek and repair the cabin. By September 17 the cabin was ready to rent again.

**Cabin 11 with new foundation, repaired porch and new concrete retaining wall along the creek.**

The sudden flood was truly an unusual experience. Perhaps it should be classified as a 100 or 500 year flood. The guests in the cabins were extremely cooperative and understanding. It was also one of those experiences where you feel that the Lord is watching out for you. We had experienced some damage, but no one was injured or killed. The rain that we received along the North Shore was part of the big weather pattern that had caused the damage in the Boundary Waters Canoe Area Wilderness the previous day. It was fortunate that the storm in the Boundary Waters came during the day when campers were not sleeping in their tents and they could see what was happening around them. At the lodge we were fortunate that the electric lights stayed on all night in spite of the heavy rains and winds. It is frightening to think about what might have happened if we had been without power at the lodge during the night or if the storm in the Boundary Waters Area had come at night.

**Butch Piepho stands by the new bridge he built during the summer of 2000. This bridge replaced the bridge near cabin 10 that washed away in the 1999 flood.**

## Cabin 14 and Other Improvements

As we approached the end of the millennium we began to make plans for more improvements at the lodge, including the building of another log cabin. Again US Bank in Duluth was helpful and we were able to refinance and get a loan for the proposed projects. Part of the financing for the new cabin came through a low interest State of Minnesota loan program which is dedicated to resort improvements. Another helpful agency was the Arrowhead Regional Economic Authority.

From our experience in building cabin 12, we felt very confident that a similar cabin would be popular with guests and improve our financial situation. We decided to make the new cabin, #14, slightly larger. The two feet in added width allowed for a bigger kitchen and a separate room for the whirlpool. The lay of the land also allowed for a large storage area under the cabin where we installed a six hundred gallon tank for the off peak heating system. This system involves heating the water in the tank with electricity during the off peak hours from 10 P.M. to about 10 am. The demand for electricity is low during these hours and the local electric cooperative sells the power at about one-third the cost of daytime electricity. The heated water then circulates through "in floor" heating pipes, as called for by thermostat settings in the living areas of the cabin. This was our first experiment with "in floor" heat and we have been very pleased with the results. Earlier we had converted the heating system in our house to the same type of off peak system, except that the hot water circulates through baseboard radiators.

**Cabin 14. Rented for the first time in late May of 2000.**

The new loan also enabled other improvements; the installation of two new energy efficient furnaces in the main lodge, new blacktopping of the driveway and parking area around the main lodge, and the extension of the roof over part of the deck of cabin 12. The new furnaces completed the upgrading of the heating systems in every building at the lodge and at the Blue Water Cafe. The main lodge, restaurant, Cascade House and Blue Water Cafe, now all had new energy efficient oil or propane furnaces and every cabin and our house at the lodge had new "off peak" storage heaters. The "off peak" heaters in all the cabins, except #14 are the type that store the heat in bricks inside radiators. These changes have resulted in safer and cleaner heating systems and a significant saving on fuel costs.

These have been the major physical changes at the lodge during the past twenty-two years. However, many, many additional, smaller improvements and maintenance projects have taken place. Some of these are: new roofing on every building, new stoves, refrigerators and dishwashing equipment in the restaurant, new storm windows on the lodge, new vehicles, lawn mowers and snowblowers, mattresses and box springs, furniture, playground equipment, computers and printers, etc. Sometimes I have explained the ongoing maintenance and repairs to the lodge as being similar to what one does at one's home. It's just that at the lodge it is like having twenty houses to care for. The list of needed repairs and desire for improvements will go on, but at this stage in the history of the lodge, it is satisfying to know that the process of winterization is complete, the transition into the computer age is on schedule and a historic place was been well maintained and we believe appropriately modernized.

In conclusion, it is interesting to look back at the accomplishments of every owner. Each owner has played a significant role in the development of a very special place. The historical records indicate that every owner worked very hard and took on considerable financial risk to make various improvements. Each new owner has built on the effort, creativity, dreams and financial investment of prior owners. The end result is a landmark on the North Shore.

It seems appropriate to end this chapter and this book with a quote from a wonderful article written by Larry Oakes in the *Minneapolis Star Tribune* about the lodge's 75 years of history. He wrote as follows:

Cascade Lodge comes into view northeast of Lutsen, where Hwy. 61 bends down for yet another hug from Lake Superior.

By then - two hours out of Duluth - the traveler is well charmed by the shore's siren song of water, rock, forest and sky, played for the eye in perfect harmony.

It faces the lake from the opposite side of the highway - a stately 2-½ story structure on a large lawn. You glance at the shutters and twin gables, the split stones and half logs, and you half expect to see a Model A roadster in the drive, suitcases strapped to its running boards.

The old place seems to belong to the landscape, like a white steeple in a New England valley, or a faded red barn in a sea of Midwestern grass.

Named for the river that tumbles there into the big lake, Cascade Lodge has had a long time to become part of the shore;… has been celebrating its 75th anniversary this year.

The milestone inspired Gene and Laurene Glader, transplanted Twin Citians who have owned the place for 21 years, to document Cascade's story. They dug through archives and interviewed old-timers.

The history of their place is intertwined with the story of how the North Shore evolved into one of Minnesota's most popular tourist destinations.[3]

---

[3] Larry Oakes, "Haven by the big lake," <u>Minneapolis Star Tribune</u>, December 22, 2002, pp. B2 & B9.

# CASCADE LODGE AND RESTAURANT

### SUMMER
**(May 1,— October 31, 2000)**

#### PEAK SEASON RATES

| | |
|---|---|
| Rooms in Main Lodge | $76.00 - 112.00 |
| Suite in lodge | $138.00 |
| Motel Units | $69.00 & 116.00 |
| Log Cabins with fireplace | $116.00 & 126.00 |
| Cabins without fireplaces | $82.00 & 90.00 |
| Cabins with fireplaces & kitchenettes | $130.00 |
| Log cabins w/ fireplaces, kitchenettes and whirlpool tubs | $155.00 & 189.00 |
| Cascade House | $200.00 |

Above rates based on double occupancy. Each additional person is $11 - $13 per night. Children under 12 years stay free with parents. Children 13 -17 years $10 with parents.

One night's lodging deposit required, applied to any unused night of reservation. Main lodge is smoke-free.

**See back panel for Discount Time Periods**

#### SENIOR CITIZEN DISCOUNT

10% daily except holidays and prime weekends. One person must be 60 or older.

#### GOLF DISCOUNTS

Special green fee rates at Superior National Golf Course when purchased with accomodations.

#### MEAL DISCOUNTS AVAILABLE

#### GROUP PACKAGES AVAILABLE!

Phone: (218) 387-1112
TOLL FREE: 1-800-322-9543
3719 W. Hwy. 61, Lutsen, MN 55612
www.cascadelodgemn.com
Owners: Gene & Laurene Glader

---

Rate Card for summer of 2000 with new format. The rate card for the summer of 1996 marked the date of change to a new format. The little pocket card was becoming too small to hold all the necessary information.

**Back and front panels of New Brochure Year in 2001. Seasonal inserts were included with the brochure when it was mailed out.**

Imagine…

crashing waves against a rocky shore, the sound of the wind through trees, the scent of pine in the air and wild flowers along the woodland trails. This isn't a dream but Cascade Lodge country — the north shore of beautiful Lake Superior.

"What a wonderful place for a lodge"
— Lake Superior Magazine

"Just steps from some of the shores most popular hiking trails"
— Midwest Living

**First two inside panels of 2001 brochure.**

The ever changing seasons open new vistas throughout the year. Early days of spring bring sounds of melting rivulets of snow, and forest floors are covered with delicate wild flowers. Days soon turn long sliding into Summer with its warm sun . . . a canopy of green, and cool quiet nights. Come Fall, the days turn crisp with the trees all aflame in red and gold. Winter is the quiet season, shhh! White, frozen and jewel like . . . the only sound is skis gliding across the pristine snow.

Nestled in the forest surrounding Cascade River State Park is Cascade Lodge, a charming 1930's lodge featured in Country Inns & America's Wonderful Little Hotels and Inns. The proximity to the State Park and the access to the Superior Hiking Trail makes Cascade Lodge unique.

The main lodge has a cozy stone fireplace and two large living rooms overlooking the lake. The lodge also serves as a focal point for the grounds and provides comfortable accommodations. An assortment of log cabins, some with fireplaces, whirlpools, kitchenettes and decks, offer a variety of conveniences to meet every taste. The Cascade House is a facility that can provide accommodations for groups large and small.

Our distinctive North Shore Restaurant & Gift Shop serves "superior" breakfasts, lunches and dinners throughout the year.

The North Shore area offers a myriad of outdoor opportunities that can meet most individuals expectations. If hiking is your desire, trails lead for miles directly from our front door. If golf is tops on your list, tee off on beautiful Superior National Golf Course. Fishing . . . of course, on rivers or lakes, both big and small. Mountain biking, kayaking and canoeing are also very popular sports in the area.

Winter season opens up a different world of opportunities. Cross country skiing, on "Piston-Bully" groomed trails right from the lodge, downhill skiing or snow-

**Inside left panels on 2001 brochure. Inside of cabin 12, outside of cabin 14 and children's play area by main lodge.**

shoeing. We have listed just a few of the things you can do throughout the year while spending time at Cascade Lodge. And, of course, you can always relax, read or just enjoy the view.

Whichever season whets your appetite Cascade Lodge is here to fill that need. Let the North Shore renew your spirit, help you see things more clearly and then return home refreshed. Give us a call and let us show you *Cascade Country*.

**Right inside panels of 2001 brochure. Pictures of Cascade Restaurant, inside of cabin 2, Superior National Golf Course, skiing at Lutsen Mt., cross country skiing behind Cascade Lodge and snowshoeing.**

# *Epilogue*

## Sale of Lodge to the O'Phelans

In early September 2003 Michael O'Phelan contacted us and asked us if the lodge was for sale. We told him we were trying to figure out how to retire and that we were open to selling the lodge. Thus began almost nine months of communication and negotiations with Maureen and Michael O'Phelan and our attorneys and accountants. The sale was consummated on May 3, 2004 at a law office in Grand Marais and another new era in the history of Cascade Lodge began.

**Michael and Maureen O'Phelan and Laurene and Gene Glader**
**at the closing on May 3, 2004.**

It has been a pleasure for Laurene and me to become acquainted with Michael and Maureen and we are so pleased to have been able to sell the resort to such fine people. It was our desire to see the lodge transition into the hands of people who share many of the same values and beliefs we hold. As we came to know the O'Phelans we discovered that we were of a kindred spirit. Consequently, it has been easy to let go of the pleasures and work of owning and managing the resort. I'm confident that as former guests return to the lodge they will find pleasure in getting to know the O'Phelans.

Michael and Maureen have brought new energy to Cascade Lodge and will undoubtedly bring new ideas to the management of the lodge. It will be interesting to observe the next few decades as they build on the foundation of previous owners.

Michael has been an engineer for over 20 years and Maureen, professionally is a lawyer, but has been primarily a wife and mother during the recent years. They have made a major career change in their forties somewhat similar to the one Laurene and I made in 1981. The O'Phelans have four children in elementary school as they make this transition in work and lifestyle. Following the sale, Laurene and I moved into a house in Grand Marais which we purchased in May of 2004. We spent twenty-three years and nine months in the resort business and we look forward to the future.

**The O'Phelan family. Front row: Samuel, Elizabeth and Shannon. Back row: Sarah, Michael and Maureen.**

# *Cascade Lodge Photographs*

**Aerial view of Cascade Lodge 2003.** *Photo by Robert J. Hurt.*

**Aerial view of Cascade Lodge looking South West.** *Photo by Robert J. Hurt.*

**Cascade Lodge from the air looking North East.** *Photo by Robert J. Hurt.*

**One of the many waterfalls on the Cascade River.**

**Left to Right: Mrs. Minnie Neudahl, Harriet Neudahl and Elvira Neudahl in back and LaVerne Neudahl in front. Circa 1935.** *Photo courtesy of Valaine Robinet.*

**Old staff cabins across the driveway from the motel.
The small cabin on the right was torn down in about 1990.**

**Restaurant, winter of 1971-72 with the new exterior color.**

**Post Card of Interior of Cabin 3.** *Circa late 1970's.*

**Narrow trails with one set track. Circa later 1970s and early 1980s.**

**Entrance to cabin 11 after a snowfall.**

**Photo of Cabins 1, 2 and 3  circa 1988.** *Photo by Richard Hamilton Smith.*

Lake Superior shoreline looking west from the lodge.

Winter at the lodge.

**A good year for snow. Mali Langlie at the lower end of the Pioneer Loop.**

**Restaurant with closeup of wagon wheel chandeliers.** *Circa 1990.*

**Inside of Cabin 7.**  Circa 1995.

**The black bears have been frequent visitors to the lodge over the years,  especially in early September. They loved the dumpsters and garbage cans.** *Circa 1990.*

**Main Lodge 1993.** *Photo by Tim Slattery.*

**A portion of room 201 in the main lodge.**

During the summer of 2000 the main driveway was blacktopped for the first time. The blacktop solved problems caused by dust and erosion.

Installing three new septic holding tanks in year 2001. One was a 5,000 gallon tank and the other two were 8,000 gallon tanks.

**Mark Delamater on new bridge he is building across the Cascade Creek on the Wild Flower Trail, Summer of 2002.**

**75ᵗʰ Anniversary Celebration Float in 2002 Fishermen's Picnic Parade in Grand Marais.** *Photo courtesy of Scott Benson.*

**New bridge to Cabin 11 built by Mark Delamater in 2003.**

**Laurene and Gene Glader 1989.**

# Appendixes

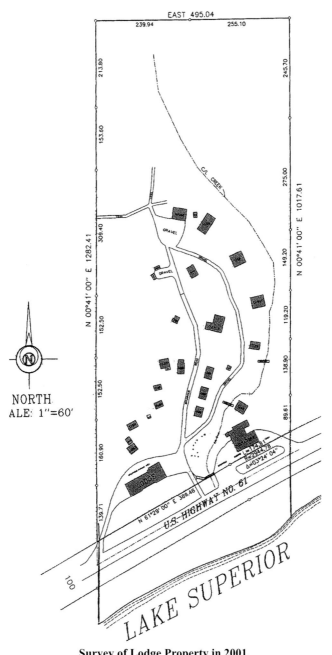

**Survey of Lodge Property in 2001.**

# Appendixes

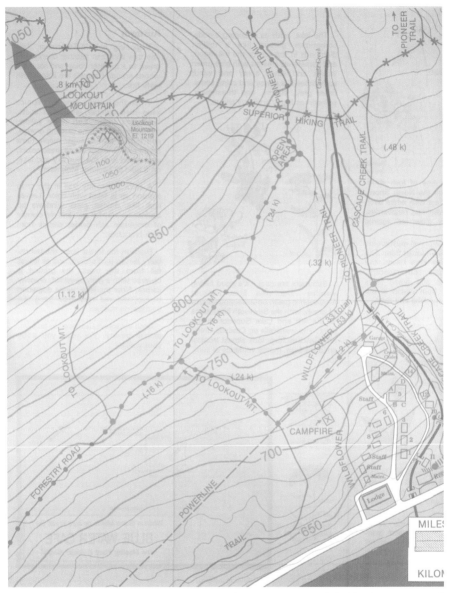

**Hiking trails around the lodge. West panels of map. Note symbols indicating segment of the Superior Hiking Trail and symbols indicating multiple use for Mountain Biking.**

224

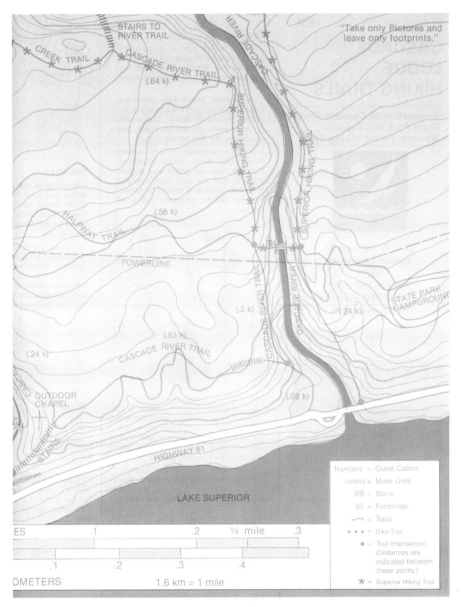

**Hiking trails around the lodge. East panels of map. Note symbols indicating segment of the Superior Hiking Trail.**

225

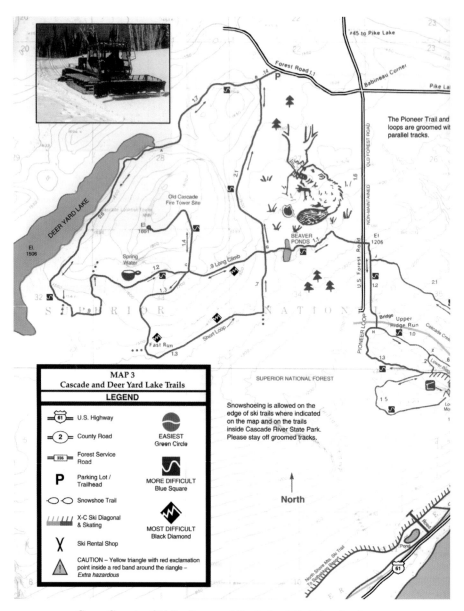

Cross Country Ski Trail around the lodge. West Panels of map.

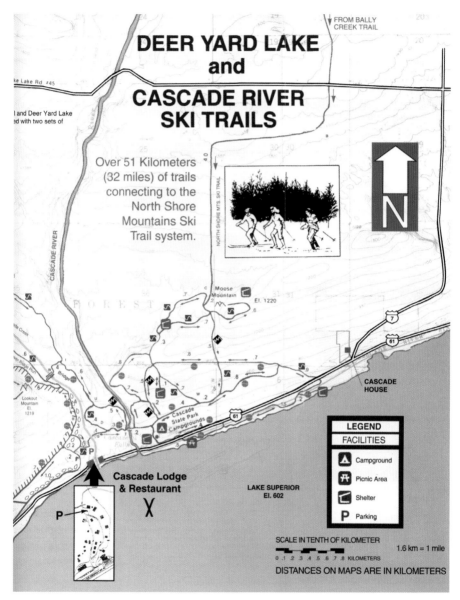

**Cross Country Ski Trail around the lodge. East Panels of map. Note trail symbols for snowshoeing.**

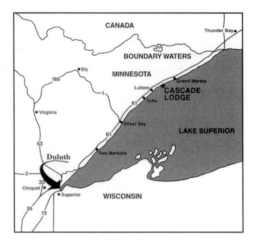

## Cascade Lodge

*Located midway between Duluth and Thunder Bay*

Cascade Lodge is just 100 miles from Duluth on Highway 61 and approximately five hours from the Twin Cities. By car or bus it is four lane freeway all the way to Two Harbors and from there one follows what many consider to be one of the most scenic drives in the country.

**Location of Cascade Lodge.**

**List of Travel Guides and Directories in which Cascade Lodge is or has been Listed:**

1. Crossette, Barbara. *America's Wonderful Little Hotels and Inns Eastern Region*. New York, NY: Congdon & Weed, Inc. Several Editions.

2. Gordon, Timothy E. and Oliveira, Ana Bela. *Gordon's Guide to Adventure Vacations*, Fresno, CA: TAG Publishing, 1998.

3. Herow, William C. *America's Scenic Drives, Travel Guide & Atlas*, Aurora, CO: Roundabout Publications, 1997.

4. Hitchcock, Anthony & Lindgren, Jean. *Country Inns Historic Hotels, The Midwest and Rocky Mountain States.* New York, NY: Burt Franklin and Company, Inc., Several Editions.

5. Kreag, Judy. *Lake Superior's North Shore, Restaurant Guide with Menus and Recipes.* Kuttawa, Kentucky  McClanahan Publishing House, Inc., 1991.

6. Noren, Elizabeth and Gary. *Ski Minnesota, A Cross Country Skier's Guide to Minnesota, Northern Wisconsin, and Michigan's Upper Peninsula.* Minneapolis, MN: Nodin Press, A Division of Mecawber, Inc., Several Editions.

7. Slade, Andrew. *White Woods, Quiet Trails: Exploring Minnesota's North Shore in Winter.* Two Harbors, Minnesota: Ridgeline Press, 1997.

8. Thaxton, John. *State and National Parks Lodges and Cabins.* New York, NY: Burt Franklin and Company, Inc., Several Editions.

9. Warner, George. *Byway Eateries of Minnesota.* Cambridge, MN: Adventure Publications, Inc., 2000.

10. Wiesel, Jonathan. *Jonathan Wiesel's Cross Country Ski Vacations, A Guide to the Best Resorts, Lodges and Groomed Trails in North America*, Sante Fe, NM: John Muir Publications, 1997.

# Appendixes